The Western Sahara Question and International Law

This book analyses recent developments concerning the application of the international legal doctrines of recognition and self-determination in relation to the Western Sahara Question. It investigates the emergent shift in favour of Morocco's sovereignty claim to Western Sahara as apparent from the positions adopted by an increasing number of third States in the United Nations and the recent spate of third States establishing consulates in Western Sahara, with Morocco's encouragement. It reflects on what the functioning of the doctrines of recognition and self-determination in this situation reveals about contemporary international law in practice more generally. The work will be of interest to scholars, researchers, and postgraduate students as well as practitioners of public international law who have a particular interest in decolonisation, self-determination disputes, and/or conflicts about natural resource entitlements. It will also appeal to readers with an interest in the work of International Organisations, including the United Nations, the European Union, and the African Union, and to specialists in international relations and regional politics.

Stephen Allen is Senior Lecturer in Law at Queen Mary, University of London, and a practising barrister.

Jamie Trinidad KC is Fellow and Director of Studies in Law at Wolfson College, University of Cambridge, Fellow of the Lauterpacht Centre for International Law, and a practising barrister.

The Western Sahara Question and International Law

Recognition Doctrine and Self-Determination

Stephen Allen and Jamie Trinidad

Routledge
Taylor & Francis Group
LONDON AND NEW YORK

First published 2024
by Routledge
4 Park Square, Milton Park, Abingdon, Oxon OX14 4RN

and by Routledge
605 Third Avenue, New York, NY 10158

Routledge is an imprint of the Taylor & Francis Group, an informa business

British Library Cataloguing-in-Publication Data
A catalogue record for this book is available from the British Library

Library of Congress Cataloging-in-Publication Data
Names: Allen, Steve, 1968- author. | Trinidad, Jamie, author.
Title: The Western Sahara question and international law : recognition doctrine and self-determination / Stephen Allen and Jamie Trinidad.
Description: Abingdon, Oxon [UK] ; New York, NY : Routledge, 2024. | Includes bibliographical references and index. | Identifiers: LCCN 2023047822 (print) | LCCN 2023047823 (ebook) | ISBN 9781032658797 (hardback) | ISBN 9781032658803 (paperback) | ISBN 9781032658827 (ebook)
Subjects: LCSH: Self-determination, National--Western Sahara. | Western Sahara--International status. | Recognition (International law) | Sovereignty. | Western Sahara--Relations--Morocco. | Morocco--Relations--Western Sahara. | Western Sahara--International status.
Classification: LCC KZ4702 .A45 2024 (print) | LCC KZ4702 (ebook) | DDC 341.4/209648--dc23/eng/20231012
LC record available at https://lccn.loc.gov/2023047822
LC ebook record available at https://lccn.loc.gov/2023047823

ISBN: 978-1-032-65879-7 (hbk)
ISBN: 978-1-032-65880-3 (pbk)
ISBN: 978-1-032-65882-7 (ebk)

DOI: 10.4324/9781032658827

Typeset in Times New Roman
by Deanta Global Publishing Services, Chennai, India

Contents

Preface

Western Sahara is the last colony on mainland Africa. In 1976, Spain withdrew its colonial administration despite an ongoing armed conflict between the Polisario Front, the Territory's national liberation movement, and Morocco. Morocco's annexation of Western Sahara began shortly thereafter, and it has controlled most of the Territory ever since. Morocco's actions were widely considered to violate those peremptory norms of international law which guard against the acquisition of territory by force and the denial of self-determination. Consequently, it was assumed that this situation generated a duty of non-recognition by which third States and International Organisations (IOs) were prohibited from recognising the lawfulness of Morocco's assertion of sovereignty over Western Sahara while being required to refrain from dealing with the Moroccan government vis-à-vis Western Sahara. This belief was strengthened by the fact that no third States or IOs officially recognised Morocco's territorial claim to Western Sahara for over 40 years. However, in recent years, third States and IOs have been increasingly willing to accommodate Morocco's sovereignty claim in ways that engage the doctrine of recognition.

This book analyses the interaction between the doctrines of recognition and self-determination in the context of the Western Sahara Question with reference to the operation of the duty of non-recognition, and by examining the consequences of the 'recognition battle' between Morocco and the Sahrawi Arab Democratic Republic over the Territory's status. The work also investigates the emergent shift in favour of Morocco's sovereignty claim to Western Sahara as apparent from the positions adopted by an increasing number of third States in the UN Security Council and/or General Assembly. In particular, this trend is evidenced by the growing support for Morocco's autonomy plan for its 'southern provinces' (Western Sahara) within the United Nations and the recent spate of third States establishing consulates in Western Sahara, with Morocco's encouragement. The book reflects on what the functioning of the doctrines of recognition and self-determination in this situation reveals about contemporary international law in practice more generally.

Acknowledgements

The authors would like to express our gratitude to Alison Kirk for all her help and advice during the publishing process. We wish to acknowledge Nektarios Papadimos (PhD candidate at the University of Vienna) for his valuable assistance in preparing the manuscript for publication. We also extend our sincere thanks to Professor Juan Soroeta for his incisive review of the draft manuscript and for his generous endorsement. Stephen Allen wishes to thank QMUL for the funding to cover the open access arrangements for this publication and Professor Jonathan Griffiths, Head of Department, for his support. Jamie Trinidad wishes to thank Wolfson College, Cambridge for its generous funding and support.

Figure 0.1 UN Map of Western Sahara (No 3691 Rev 95)

1 Introduction

Morocco has long claimed that Western Sahara – the last colony on mainland Africa – constitutes an integral part of its national territory. It advances this claim notwithstanding the General Assembly's insistence that a referendum of the people of this Non-Self-Governing Territory (NSGT or Territory), formerly known as 'Spanish Sahara', be held to bring about its decolonisation.[1] The applicability of the principle of self-determination in Western Sahara, and the absence of sovereign ties between Morocco and the Territory, were confirmed by the International Court of Justice (ICJ) in its 1975 *Western Sahara* Advisory Opinion.[2]

If one accepts the ICJ's conclusion that the right to self-determination is vested in the Sahrawi people as a matter of international law, it follows that Morocco's subsequent occupation of Western Sahara, in violation of the peremptory norms concerning the prohibition on the use of force and the right to self-determination, has generated *erga omnes* obligations (that is to say, obligations 'towards the community of States as a whole')[3] for third States and International Organisations (IOs), which are under a duty to withhold recognition of Morocco's assertion of sovereignty and to refrain from dealing with it vis-à-vis Western Sahara.[4] Indeed, such a collective obligation has been readily assumed to exist in this setting by reference to the applicable

1 See e.g., UNGA Res 2072 (XX) (1965), 2229 (XXI) (1966), 2345 (XXII) (1967), 2428 (XXIII) (1968), 3162 (XXVIII) (1973), and 3292 (XXIX) (1974).

2 *Western Sahara* (Advisory Opinion) (1975) *ICJ Rep 12*, paras 59 and 162.

3 *Barcelona Traction, Light and Power Company, Limited (Belgium v. Spain) (New Application: 1962)* (Judgment – Second Phase) (1970) *ICJ Rep 3*, 32, para 33.

4 See Articles 40–42 of the Articles on Responsibility of States for International Wrongful Acts (ARSIWA). According to Article 41(2), 'No State shall recognize as lawful a situation created by a serious breach within the meaning of Article 40, nor render aid or assistance in maintaining that situation'. The definition of a 'serious breach' in Article 40 is 'a breach by a State of an obligation arising under a peremptory norm of international law' that 'involves a gross or systematic failure by the responsible State to fulfil the obligation'. See also Articles 41 and 42(2), Draft Articles on the Responsibility of International Organisations (DARIO). Also, James Crawford, *State Responsibility: The General Part* (CUP 2013) 381–385, and in particular at 382 (citing the views of Blix (1970) and Dinstein (2011)): 'the application of the obligation of non-recognition is uncertain, but the thrust of the international law position is that in the event of annexation leading to the

DOI: 10.4324/9781032658827-1

customary international law,[5] and the fact that no third State (or IO) formally recognised Morocco's sovereignty claim to Western Sahara for over 40 years would seem to support this interpretation.[6] However, it is sometimes argued that a duty of non-recognition cannot emerge in a concrete case without prior authorisation from the Security Council (or ICJ).[7] It is notable that none of the United Nation's (UN's) principal organs have declared the existence of a duty of non-recognition in response to the situation prevailing in Western Sahara.[8] The fact that third States and IOs (such as the European Union) chose to withhold recognition of Morocco's territorial claim may have been indicative of their attitude to Morocco's wrongdoing in that Territory rather than in response to a legally binding obligation. In such circumstances, this book considers how the duty of non-recognition is triggered and whether one has emerged in relation to Western Sahara and examines the legal consequences that would flow from the existence of such an obligation.

While the focus of the book will be on the international legal dimensions of the Western Sahara Question, these cannot be abstracted from the stark realities on the ground in the Territory and the broader political context. After years of armed conflict, the Security Council and the Organisation of African Unity (OAU) brokered the 1988 Settlement Proposals by which Morocco and the Polisario Front agreed to a ceasefire and the holding of a referendum of the

continuous and effective control of territory by an aggressor, no prescriptive rights may evolve in favour of the aggressor, or be recognized by the international community' (footnotes omitted).

5 See the judgment of the African Court of Human and Peoples' Rights in the *Bernard Mornah Case* (22 September 2022) for recent authoritative evidence of this assumption (discussed in Chapter III(D)(ii) below).

6 It also has wide academic support: see e.g., the 2022 'Statement on Western Sahara and International Law' issued by the Spanish Association of Professors of International Law and International Relations (AEPDIRI), signed by several hundred academics after the Spanish government's decision to back the Moroccan autonomy plan, in particular para 7 on the duty of non-recognition, AEPDIRI, 'Declaración Sobre El Sahara Occidental Y El Derecho Internacional' <https://www.aepdiri.org/index.php/actividades-aepdiri/declaracion-sahara> accessed 31 August 2023. Also, Anne Lagerwall and Tom Ruys, 'Special Issue: Western Sahara on the Edges of International Law: Introduction' (2020) 2 *Revue Belge de Droit International* 381, and other contributions to that Special Issue, including the 'Keynote Address' of Hans Corell (at 423) former Legal Counsel to the UN who in 2002 advised the Security Council on the legality of certain contracts signed by Morocco with companies for the exploitation of mineral resources in Western Sahara. Also, Isaías Barreñada and Raquel Ojeda (eds), *Sahara Occidental: 40 años después* (Madrid: Catarata 2016). It is difficult to find international law scholarship that is supportive of the view that Morocco is sovereign over the territory it refers to as its 'southern provinces', other than work by Moroccan scholars, e.g., the two-volume study by Abdelhamid el Ouali, *Le conflit du Sahara au regard du droit international* (Brussels: Bruylant 2015).

7 See Chapter III(A) below.

8 Cf UNSC Res 277 (18 March 1970) calling on UN Member States not to recognise the 'illegal regime' in Southern Rhodesia, and UNSC Res 541 (18 November 1983) calling on Member States not to recognise the 'legally invalid' declaration of independence of the 'Turkish Republic of Northern Cyprus'.

Territory's inhabitants to be organised by the UN. However, a referendum has never been held and a negotiated political solution to the dispute providing for the self-determination of the people of Western Sahara has proved to be elusive, despite the Security Council's close involvement. Morocco's entrenched control over most of the Territory; partisanship among the Council's membership; and the collapse of the 30-year ceasefire in November 2020 leading to the resumption of armed conflict have coincided to change the dynamics of the dispute in fundamental ways.

This book examines the increasing willingness, on the part of certain third States and IOs, to accept Morocco's territorial claim to Western Sahara either by way of their bilateral dealings with the Moroccan government or via the adoption of increasingly sympathetic positions in international fora, such as the Security Council and General Assembly. Indirect support is apparent from the prevalence, and growing momentum, of the argument that Morocco's autonomy plan provides the *only* solution to the Western Sahara Question. Some States have gone further by recognising Morocco's sovereignty claim expressly. A move towards recognition is also evident from the recent trend of third States establishing consulates in Western Sahara. This book analyses these related developments and asks whether such activity amounts to implied recognition of Morocco's sovereignty claim.

As will be seen, Morocco has skilfully exploited the opportunity to advance its cause through various diplomatic means, including through the adoption of regional investment strategies, the promotion of human rights initiatives at 'home' and abroad as well as through the pursuit of COVID-19 diplomacy. It has also intensified its application of the 'Hallstein doctrine' in recent years to bring about an ebb in third-State recognition of its competitor, the Sahrawi Arab Democratic Republic (SADR), which was unilaterally declared by the Polisario in 1976.[9] By adopting this strategy, Morocco has succeeded in constraining third-State recognition of the SADR over the years by either pressuring States to withdraw their recognition, to 'suspend' or 'freeze' it, or to prevent it from being granted at all. Against this background, this book contemplates whether Morocco is on the path to acquiring good title to Western Sahara and asks what such an outcome might reveal about the content and operation of the doctrines of self-determination and recognition in contemporary international law.

Chapter 2 will look at the historical background to the Western Sahara Question, with a focus on the UN General Assembly's early involvement, the ICJ's *Western Sahara* Advisory Opinion, and the UN Security Council's

9 This doctrine involves a State threatening to withdraw (or withhold) recognition from a third State/government which has, or is planning, to recognise its rival and it is often characterised by a 'carrot-and-stick' approach. See Thomas D Grant, 'The Hallstein Doctrine and Regimes of Non-Recognition' (2000) 36 *StanJIntlL* 221.

initial engagement with the dispute (A) before addressing the recognition practices surrounding the purported statehood of the SADR (B).

Chapter 3 will discuss various aspects of the duty of non-recognition with reference to developments in Western Sahara. After addressing doctrinal questions around the non-recognition doctrine (A) and the discretionary character of recognition (B), the chapter will proceed to discuss the notion of formalism and implied recognition by reference to the legal controversies surrounding the EU/Morocco Trade and Fishing Agreements and their putative application in Western Sahara. The chapter then turns to the consequences of the duty of non-recognition (C), with reference to persistent illegal situations and territorial claims, and to the 2022 judgment of the African Court of Human and Peoples' Rights in the *Bernard Mornah* Case.[10]

Chapter 4 will analyse recent developments in UN practice in relation to Western Sahara. To this end, it will examine the Security Council's approach since 2018 (A), and the approach of the General Assembly and its subsidiary organs, the Special Committee on Decolonisation ('C24') and Fourth Committee, since 2020 (B).

Chapter 5 will examine recent State practice beyond the UN and explore the possible legal ramifications of growing support among States for the Moroccan autonomy plan (A), and an accompanying recent spike in the establishment of consulates by States which are sympathetic to Morocco's sovereignty claim in Western Sahara (B).

The book's conclusion considers the possibility of a future change in the status of Western Sahara that is opposed by the Sahrawi people, and what this could mean for the future of international law itself, in particular the peremptory norms on self-determination and territorial integrity that currently underpin the decolonisation process. Such principles, it is suggested, have a load-bearing character within the legal and political architecture of the UN system, beyond the decolonisation context, and their erosion in the case of Western Sahara could come to be seen as emblematic of a 21st-century shift away from a rules-based international order.

10 *Bernard Mornah v Benin et al* (judgment 22 September 2022).

2 Self-Determination and the Western Sahara Question

The right to self-determination in international law is particularly susceptible to the charge of indeterminacy.[1] Nevertheless, it did acquire a definite meaning and application in relation to the process of decolonisation. The right's assured content in this context arose because it was assumed that the territorial integrity of the colonial units forged by European colonialism in Africa, Asia, and elsewhere would form the structural basis for decolonisation, notwithstanding the well-documented artificiality of colonial boundaries.[2] Consequently, the right to self-determination would be exercised by the people of a given colonial unit, with the notion of peoplehood having a territorial expression for this purpose.[3]

Since the 1950s, the UN General Assembly has played a leading role in devising the policy by which the scourge of colonialism was to be eradicated as well as overseeing its implementation in discrete cases. This institutional action led to the development and consolidation of a body of customary international law, which facilitated and shaped the process of widespread decolonisation that occurred from the 1960s onwards.[4] Decolonisation enabled the people concerned to choose their future political status from several options, namely: independence as a sovereign State; free association with a State (typically, the former colonial power); integration with a State; or any other political status freely chosen by them.[5] The standard method of ascertaining the

1 As James Crawford observed, even the *lex lata* of self-determination is *lex obscura*, in James Crawford, 'The Right to Self-Determination in International Law: Its Development and Future', in Philip Alston (ed) *Peoples Rights* (OUP 2001) 7, 38. See also Martti Koskenniemi, 'National Self-Determination' (1994) 43 *ICLQ* 241.

2 This standpoint was sustained by the principle of *uti possidetis juris* which created a presumption that the boundaries of colonial administrative units would become the international frontiers of a newly independent State in the event of decolonisation. This was expressed in the African context as the inviolability of received frontiers.

3 Colonial entities were classified as either Non-Self-Governing or Trust Territories under Articles 73 and 76 of the UN Charter.

4 UNGA Res 1514 (XV) (14 December 1960); 1541 (XV) (15 December 1960) ('Colonial Declaration'); and 2625 (XXV) (24 October 1970) ('Declaration on Friendly Relations').

5 ibid.

DOI: 10.4324/9781032658827-2

freely expressed will of the people was through the holding of a referendum on the basis of universal suffrage.[6]

Spain initially resisted the UN's efforts to identify 'Spanish Sahara' (Western Sahara or Rio de Oro and Sakiet El Hamra) as a NSGT, pursuant to the rights and obligations contained in Chapter XI of the UN Charter.[7] However, by 1961, the Spanish government had acknowledged that Western Sahara, along with Spain's other African colonies – namely Ifni, a former Spanish exclave lying a short distance north of Western Sahara, and Spanish Guinea (later Equatorial Guinea) – were NSGTs and it undertook to transmit information on them, in accordance with the reporting requirements contained in Article 73(e) of the UN Charter.[8] In 1963, the General Assembly listed Western Sahara as a NSGT,[9] and the Spanish government subsequently declared itself in favour of the Territory's inhabitants exercising their right to self-determination.[10] However, Morocco claimed to have exercised sovereignty over Rio de Oro and Sakiet El Hamra before they came under the control of the Spanish colonial authorities. Soon after it had achieved its independence from French and Spanish colonial rule in 1956, Morocco sought to recover Western Sahara. It argued that the international law concerning decolonisation could not affect the restoration of its territorial integrity. Mauritania maintained a similar claim over Western Sahara's southern reaches. Against this backdrop, the so-called 'Western Sahara Question' became a matter of international concern and controversy.

6 According to Resolution 1541 (XV) (1960), the options of free association and integration required a free expression of the popular will 'through informed and democratic processes' (Principles VII and IX). However, a plebiscite was not strictly required. For instance, the Cook Islands became freely associated with New Zealand in 1965 after elections to the territory's Legislative Assembly and a vote by that body in favour of the new constitutional arrangement. Several States have acceded to independence without a referendum (e.g., Cyprus, Namibia, Mauritius, and Belize).

7 On 10 November 1958, the Spanish government advised the UN Secretary-General that any African territories subject to its sovereignty were Spanish provinces under its municipal law. *Western Sahara* (Advisory Opinion) [1975] *ICJ Rep* 12, para 34.

8 *Western Sahara* (Advisory Opinion), para. 35. Spain has always maintained that the North African exclaves of Ceuta, Melilla, Vélez de la Gomera, Alhucemas, and the Chafarinas Islands are integral parts of Spain, and it did not list them as NSGTs, notwithstanding Morocco's claims to those territories: see Jamie Trinidad, 'An Evaluation of Morocco's Claims to Spain's Remaining Territories in Africa' (2012) 61 *ICLQ* 4, 961.

9 UNGA 'Report of the Committee of Information from Non-Self-Governing Territories' (XVIII) (1963) UN A/5514, Annex III, 34.

10 See the Special Committee on the Situation regarding the Implementation of the Declaration on the Granting of Independence to Colonial Countries and Peoples (C24), Report A/6300/Rev. 1 (1966) 604.

A. UN and ICJ Involvement up to the Creation of the SADR in 1976

(i) The General Assembly's Early Involvement (1963–1974)

Between 1965 and 1974, the General Assembly adopted a series of resolutions addressing the arrangements for the Territory's decolonisation.[11] In particular, through Resolution 2229 (XXI) (1966), the Assembly: 'Reaffirm[ed] the inalienable right of the peoples of Ifni and Spanish Sahara to self-determination in accordance with General Assembly Resolution 1514 (XV)'.[12] Moreover, it:

> Invite[d] the administering Power to determine at the earliest possible date, in conformity with the aspirations of the indigenous people of Spanish Sahara and in consultation with the Governments of Mauritania and Morocco and any other interested party, the procedures for the holding of a referendum under United Nations auspices with a view to enabling the indigenous population of the Territory to exercise freely its right to self-determination and, to this end:
>
> (a) To create a favourable climate for the referendum to be conducted on an entirely free, democratic and impartial basis, by permitting, inter alia, the return of exiles to the Territory;
> (b) To take all the necessary steps to ensure that only the indigenous people of the Territory participate in the referendum;
> (c) To refrain from any action likely to delay the process of the decolonization of Spanish Sahara;
> (d) To provide all the necessary facilities to a United Nations mission so that it may be able to participate actively in the organization and holding of the referendum.[13]

General Assembly Resolutions 2345 (XXII) (1967), 2428 (XXIII) (1968), and 3162 (XXVIII) (1973) followed along the same lines.[14] Together, they confirmed that the Assembly's approach to the decolonisation of Western Sahara would be to allow the Territory's people to exercise their right of self-determination by means of the holding of a free and fair democratic referendum, organised under the auspices of the UN.

11 Starting with UNGA Res 2072 (XX) (1965).

12 UNGA Res 2229 (XXI), 20 December 1966, para 1.

13 ibid., para 4. Spain ceded Ifni to Morocco in 1969 without a referendum being held. The General Assembly adopted different approaches in relation to Ifni and Western Sahara. See, e.g., UNGA Res 2229 (XXI), para 3 (which refers to a 'transfer of powers' from Spain to Morocco, 'bearing in mind the aspirations of the indigenous population' of Ifni) and para 4, and the *Western Sahara* (Advisory Opinion), paras 59–63. For discussion, see Jamie Trinidad, *Self-Determination in Disputed Colonial Territories* (CUP 2018) 56–66.

14 *Western Sahara* (Advisory Opinion), paras 63 and 64.

It is apparent from the series of resolutions referred to above that Spain was in no hurry to withdraw from the Territory, a fact that may be explained by the discovery of rich deposits of phosphate which Spain had begun to exploit in the 1960s.[15] However, under international pressure, Spain conducted a census of the Territory's inhabitants in 1974, a process which led to the announcement of its intention to hold a referendum regarding the Territory's future status.[16] Morocco and Mauritania lobbied against such a move in the General Assembly in a concerted effort to delay, or prevent, such a plebiscite from taking place.[17] They pushed for the Assembly to request an Advisory Opinion concerning the historical status of Western Sahara – rather than the more contentious issue of who had sovereign entitlements to the Territory in the event of its decolonisation.[18] Such an approach proved to be attractive to Morocco and Mauritania given their persistent irredentist claims to the Territory. In a surprising move, the Assembly called on Spain to postpone its planned referendum pending the outcome of the advisory proceedings.[19] It also asked the C24 to send a fact-finding visiting mission to the Territory with the instruction to report back before the Assembly's next session.[20] Nevertheless, despite choosing to embark on the unusual course of action of delaying decolonisation in a specific situation,[21] the Assembly was careful to reaffirm its commitment to the principles set out in Resolution 1514 (XV) (1960),[22] and to make sure that the questions posed in the request for an Advisory Opinion were without prejudice to their application in this setting.[23]

(ii) The UN's Visiting Mission and the Western Sahara Advisory Opinion

The Visiting Mission was tasked with reporting on the prevailing conditions in the Territory and ascertaining the wishes and aspirations of its people and

15 Antonio Cassese, *Self-Determination of Peoples: A Legal Reappraisal* (CUP 1995) 215.

16 Spain announced this course of action in a letter dated 20 August 1974 addressed to the UN Secretary-General. UN Doc. A/9714 (1974). Franck indicated that, until this point, the Moroccan government was labouring under the impression that Spain would have eventually agreed to the integration of Western Sahara into Morocco despite the content of General Assembly resolutions on Western Sahara. See Thomas Franck, 'The Stealing of the Sahara' (1976) 70 *AJIL* 4, 694, 705.

17 In September 1974, Morocco tried to obtain Spain's agreement to take their dispute over the Spanish Sahara to the ICJ as a contentious case without success. See *Western Sahara* (Advisory Opinion) paras 29, 36, and 38.

18 UNGA Res 3292 (XXIX) (13 December 1974) para 1.

19 ibid., para 3.

20 ibid., para 5.

21 See Gino Naldi, 'Western Sahara: Suspended Statehood or Frustrated Self-determination' (2005) 13 *AfrYIL* 11–41.

22 UNGA Res 3292 (XXIX) (n 18), Preamble.

23 ibid., para 1.

it visited the main population centres in Western Sahara between 8 May and 9 June 1974.[24] In its unanimous report, which was published just before the ICJ's Advisory Opinion was delivered, the Mission concluded that Saharans living in Western Sahara were overwhelmingly in favour of independence and against integration with the Territory's neighbouring States.[25] This conclusion underpinned the Mission's key recommendation – that a popular consultation involving all those Saharans originating in the Territory was needed in order to bring about the Territory's decolonisation.[26] To that end, it recommended that 'the General Assembly should take steps to enable those population groups to decide their own future in complete freedom and in an atmosphere of peace and security'.[27]

The Mission was also given the responsibility of ascertaining the views of those Saharans who originated in the Territory but who now lived outside it. This task was complicated by uncertainty surrounding the concept of 'Saharans originating in the Territory', as a result of the nomadic character of the tribes traversing the Sahara, but also given the population movements that had occurred between Western Sahara and Southern Morocco (including the Tarfaya Strip) during the 1950s and 1960s.[28] This prompted the Mission to reflect on the knotty question of who should be considered to be 'Saharans originating in the Territory'.[29]

In its *Western Sahara* Advisory Opinion, the ICJ was clearly mindful of certain qualifications as to the nature and scope of the General Assembly's request. It observed that the request had to be interpreted in the light of the provisions of General Assembly Resolution 3292 and the resolutions which led up to that point, combined with the Assembly's general policy on decolonisation and the legal principles associated with that process.[30] The Court took the view that there was nothing in Resolution 3292 to suggest the Assembly intended to deviate from the approach it had adopted to the decolonisation of Western Sahara and, in particular, its view that the people of the Territory would decide its political status through the expression of their free will in

24 See Franck (n 16) 707.

25 See Visiting Mission's Report, annexed to C24's Report of the Thirtieth Session, Vol III, A/10023, Rev 1 (1975) 48, 55; ibid., 708.

26 ibid., 9.

27 ibid., 11; Franck (n 16) 709.

28 Morocco has stressed that Moroccan nationals who arrived in the Territory as part of those population movements, and who now make up a majority of the Territory's inhabitants, should be allowed to participate in any UN-sponsored referendum concerning the final status of Western Sahara. See Chapter II(A)(iii) below for discussion.

29 In its *Western Sahara* Advisory Opinion, the ICJ seemed to appreciate the difficulty of establishing the extent to which nomadic tribal groups could be viewed as belonging to the Territory. See Franck's discussion at 697. See also Karen Knop, *Diversity and Self-Determination in International Law* (CUP 2002) 134–135, and more generally 110–167.

30 *Western Sahara* (Advisory Opinion), para 53.

accordance with the right to self-determination.[31] Nonetheless, the Court appreciated that an Advisory Opinion clarifying the legal status of Western Sahara at the time of its colonisation by Spain may assist the Assembly insofar as its continuing discussions about the Territory's decolonisation were concerned.[32] Therefore, while the Assembly had consistently endorsed the holding of a referendum through which the people of Western Sahara could exercise their right to self-determination in its previous resolutions, the Court recognised that, '[t]he right of self-determination leaves the General Assembly a measure of discretion with respect to the forms and procedures by which the right is to be realized'.[33] It acknowledged that the 'various possibilities' for Assembly action could extend 'to consultations between the interested States, and to the procedures and guarantees required for ensuring a free and genuine expression of the will of the people'.[34] Ultimately, the ICJ found that neither Morocco nor Mauritania enjoyed precolonial ties to Western Sahara that could be equated to territorial sovereignty as a matter of international law.[35] Consequently, it concluded that neither Morocco nor Mauritania's contemporary claims to Western Sahara could affect the process of decolonising the Territory, which needed to be carried out in conformity with the principle of self-determination,[36] an entitlement that was exercisable through the freely expressed will of the people of Western Sahara.[37]

In the wake of the Advisory Opinion, Morocco somehow maintained that the Court had endorsed its view that the 'so-called Western Sahara was part of Moroccan territory',[38] and King Hassan II declared his intention to organise a religiously inspired march which would involve a large group of Moroccan civilians walking into Western Sahara for the purpose of (re)claiming it for Morocco. The Spanish government urgently brought the matter to the attention of the Security Council, which called on Morocco not to proceed with its planned march.[39] However, after some delay, the Moroccan authorities

31 ibid., para 70. This was acknowledged within Resolution 3292 itself.

32 *Western Sahara* (Advisory Opinion), para 72.

33 ibid., para 71.

34 ibid., para 72. During this period, the General Assembly treated Morocco, Mauritania, and Spain as interested or concerned States. See UNGA Res 2229 (XXI) (20 December 1966), para 4.

35 *Western Sahara* (Advisory Opinion), paras 58 and 162.

36 See Declaration on the Granting of Independence to Colonial Countries and Peoples, UNGA Res 1514 (XV) (14 December 1960); Principles which should guide members in determining whether or not an obligation exists to transmit the information called for under Article 73(e) of the Charter, UNGA Res 1541 (XV) (15 December 1960); Declaration on Principles of International Law concerning Friendly Relations and Co-operation among States in accordance with the Charter of the United Nations, UNGA Res 2625 (XXV) (24 October 1970).

37 The ICJ defined the right of self-determination as 'the need to pay regard to the freely expressed will of peoples', in *Western Sahara* (Advisory Opinion), para 59.

38 Press release of the Permanent Mission of Morocco to the UN, 16 October 1975, quoted in UN Doc S/PV.1849 (1975) 11.

39 See SCR 377 (22 October 1975); and SCR 379 (2 November 1975).

instigated what became known as the 'Green March', which involved an estimated 350,000 unarmed civilians walking into the Western Sahara unopposed by the Spanish colonial authorities. In Resolution 380 (1975), the Security Council 'deplored' the march and called on Morocco to bring it to an end with immediate effect.[40]

Resolution 380 licensed the holding of negotiations by any concerned and interested parties which might resolve the Western Sahara Question as the situation posed a risk to international peace and security.[41] This prompted negotiations between Spain, Morocco, and Mauritania regarding the Territory's fate.[42] These talks produced the 'Madrid Accords', through which Spain agreed to introduce an interim administration of Western Sahara pending its withdrawal from the Territory, leaving it to be partitioned between Morocco and Mauritania along agreed lines.[43] Under the Accords, the parties maintained their commitment to consult with the Saharan populations originating in the Territory with a view to respecting their collective opinion regarding the future of Western Sahara. However, they stipulated that their will was to be expressed through the Assembly of the *Yema'a* rather than by holding a plebiscite.[44] At the time, Spain claimed that the Accords derived their legitimacy from the terms of Security Council Resolution 380 as these tripartite negotiations flowed from the Council's recommendations.[45] Moreover, the parties asserted that the Accords were concluded in a manner that upheld the principles enshrined in the UN Charter.[46]

40 See SCR 380 (6 November 1975). The Moroccan King decided to call off the Green March after it had achieved its symbolic purpose.

41 ibid.

42 UN Secretary-General's Second Report on the situation concerning Spanish Sahara, S/11876, 12 November 1975, para 3.

43 See the Declaration of Principles on Western Sahara by Spain, Morocco, and Mauritania, 14 November 1975, 988 UNTS 259; and the UNSG's Third Report on the situation concerning Spanish Sahara, 19 November 1975, S/118801, Annex 1.

44 Paragraph 3 of the Madrid Accords provides that, 'The views of the Saharan population, expressed through the *Yema'a*, will be respected'. The *Yema'a* (*Djemaa*) was a body of tribal chiefs and representatives created by Spain in 1967 in an effort to show the UN that indigenous Saharans were being consulted on certain matters connected with the Territory's administration. Although the *Yema'a* had no political power, it played a controversial legitimising role until it resolved to dissolve itself in late November 1975. See Tony Hodges, *Western Sahara: The Roots of a Desert War* (1983) 141–143 and Erik Jensen, *Western Sahara: Anatomy of a Stalemate?* (2nd ed, Lynne Rienner Publishers 2012) 18–19.

45 Juan Soroeta Liceras, *International Law and the Western Sahara Conflict* (Wolf Legal Publishers, Tilburg 2014) 126, and see SCR 380 above (n 40).

46 See Soroeta (n 45) 126–127. See also Edi Rexhaj, 'Western Sahara: Africa's Last Colony', unpublished master's thesis at the University of St Gallen (2023) 26–34, casting doubt on the validity of the Madrid Accords when viewed through the prism of the ICJ's finding in the *Chagos* Advisory Opinion that 'heightened scrutiny should be given to the issue of consent in a situation where a part of a non-self-governing territory is separated to create a new colony' [2019] *ICJ Rep* 95, para 172.

The General Assembly's response to the *Western Sahara* Advisory Opinion was a bifurcated one, resulting in the adoption of two largely contradictory resolutions.[47] In Resolution 3548A (1975), the Assembly reaffirmed the inalienable right to self-determination of the people of Western Sahara in keeping with its previous resolutions.[48] It took note of the ICJ's *Western Sahara* Advisory Opinion, with appreciation,[49] while endorsing the conclusion of the Visiting Mission's 1975 Report – that measures were needed: 'to enable all Saharans originating in the Territory to decide on their future in complete freedom and in an atmosphere of peace and security, in accordance with Resolution 1514 (XV)'.[50] This resolution, therefore, reaffirmed the Assembly's concern to ensure that the principle of self-determination was applied within a framework that would guarantee the Territory's inhabitants the opportunity to express their will in a free and genuine manner.[51] It also called upon Spain, 'to take immediately all necessary measures, in consultation with all the parties concerned and interested,[52] so that all Saharans originating in the Territory may exercise fully and freely, under United Nations supervision, [this] inalienable right'.[53]

In sharp contrast, in Resolution 3548B, the Assembly took note of the Madrid Accords,[54] before reaffirming the inalienable right to self-determination, 'of all the Saharan populations originating in the Territory' in line with Resolution 1514 (XV).[55] In this resolution, the Assembly asked the interim administration, anticipated under the tripartite Accords, to ensure that those Saharan populations 'originating in the territory will be able to exercise their inalienable right to self-determination through free consultations organized with the assistance of a [UN] representative.'[56] Although, in Resolution 3458B, the Assembly called upon the parties to the Madrid Accords 'to ensure respect for the freely expressed aspirations of the Saharan populations',[57] it foresaw that any such 'free consultations' would not need to satisfy the measures required for all Saharans originating in the Territory to exercise fully and

47 See UNGA Res 3458A and 3458B (XXX) (10 December 1975).

48 UNGA Res 3458A (XXX) (1975), para 1.

49 ibid., para 4.

50 ibid., para 5.

51 ibid., para 2. This paragraph replicates the General Assembly's statement in UNGA Res 3162 (XXVIII) (1973).

52 The interested parties were Spain, Morocco, and Mauritania, while Algeria was considered a concerned party. This approach was also followed by the Security Council in SCR 377 (22 October 1975). See Franck (n 16) 712.

53 UNGA Res 3458A, para 7.

54 See the Declaration of Principles on Western Sahara by Spain, Morocco, and Mauritania, 14 November 1975, 988 UNTS 259. Res 3458B (XXX) (10 December 1975), para 1. It also noted the ICJ's *Western Sahara* Advisory Opinion and the Visiting Mission's Report (n 25) Preamble.

55 UNGA Res 3548B, para 2.

56 ibid., para 4.

57 ibid., para 3.

freely their right to self-determination under UN supervision, as anticipated in Resolution 3458A. In other words, it did not endorse the view that a referendum would be required for the right to self-determination to be satisfied in this context.

However, the arrangements negotiated in the Accords were soon overtaken by events on the ground. By the end of 1975, Morocco and Mauritania had forcibly occupied parts of Western Sahara and they each engaged in an armed conflict with the Polisario Front – the Territory's national liberation movement – in relation to those areas which they controlled.[58] Many Sahrawis fled Western Sahara, finding refuge in neighbouring Algeria. In late February 1976, King Hassan II of Morocco sought to bring together a rump of the *Yema'a* to validate the purported free consultation process stipulated in the Accords. However, this proved to be a step too far for the Spanish government, which chose to withdraw, informing the UN Secretary-General of its decision to terminate its administration of the Territory forthwith.[59] It explained that circumstances beyond its control had prevented the organisation of a popular consultation, as required under the terms of the Madrid Accords.[60] Such developments meant that the legal requirements set out in the Madrid Accords for the transfer of Western Sahara from Spain to Morocco and Mauritania were never satisfied, notwithstanding the existence of grave doubts about their validity in any event.[61] In response, Spain made an accelerated withdrawal from the territory in February 1976 while purporting to renounce its responsibility as Western Sahara's administering power.[62]

The General Assembly's contradictory approach to the Western Sahara Question persisted for some time thereafter. For example, paragraphs 2 and 3 of Resolution 33/31A (1978) reaffirmed the people of Western Sahara's inalienable right to self-determination and independence along with the UN's responsibility to bring about the Territory's decolonisation in accordance with the principles set out in the Charter and Resolution 1514 (XV).[63] However, while the preamble of competing Resolution 33/31B (1978) recalled the

58 See Hodges (n 44) 210–228; and Toby Shelley, *Endgame in the Western Sahara* (Zed Books 2004) 26–48.

59 Spain purported to renounce its role as the administering power in a 'Letter dated 26 February 1976 from the Permanent Representative of Spain to the UN addressed to the UN Secretary-General' (26 February 1976) UN Doc A/31/56-S/11997. The Polisario declared unilateral independence in the form of the Sahrawi Arab Democratic Republic (SADR) in response.

60 See Franck (n 16) 718; Soroeta (n 45) 132–133.

61 As the Opinion of Hans Corell, Legal Counsel to the UN, to the Security Council pointed out, the Accords did not transfer sovereignty to Morocco and the UN still regards Spain as the Territory's administering power: Letter dated 29 January 2002 from the Under-Secretary-General for Legal Affairs, the Legal Counsel, addressed to the President of the Security Council', UN Doc S/2002/161.

62 Letter of 26 February 1976 (n 59).

63 See e.g., UNGA Res 33/31 (13 December 1978).

Assembly's resolutions on decolonisation in general, it failed to mention the right to self-determination explicitly and focused exclusively on the Organisation of African Unity's (OAU's) embryonic initiatives concerning Western Sahara before inviting the OAU to 'take prompt action to find a just and equitable settlement to the question of Western Sahara'.[64] Events on the ground rendered the continuation of the General Assembly's dual approach untenable.

During this period, the Polisario's guerrilla campaigns proved to be remarkably successful, especially against the military forces and interests of Mauritania, prompting it to sue for peace.[65] Consequently, on 10 August 1979, the Polisario concluded a peace treaty with Mauritania, which signalled the latter's withdrawal from the conflict.[66] However, in response, Morocco extended its control over those areas of Western Sahara formerly held by Mauritania. The General Assembly '[d]eeply deplored' such aggravating behaviour;[67] and it began to take a firmer and more unified position on the dispute, choosing to characterise Morocco's presence in Western Sahara as an 'occupation' for the first time.[68] It also acknowledged the Polisario as the legitimate representative of the people of Western Sahara and it supported the Polisario's full participation in any search for a definitive settlement of the Western Sahara Question.[69]

The Polisario also inflicted significant Moroccan casualties during their protracted military conflict, but Morocco had much greater resources at its disposal than Mauritania and the recovery of Western Sahara remained a high priority for its leadership, largely for domestic political reasons.[70] Consequently, the Moroccan government was prepared to endure the losses while it sought a military solution to the conflict. Even though the Assembly's attitude towards Morocco was hardening, it still urged Morocco to terminate its occupation of the Territory and to join the peace process.[71] To that end, in Resolution 35/19 (1980), the Assembly implored Morocco and the Polisario

64 ibid., para 3.

65 See Hodges (n 44) 241–246 and 257–278.

66 Mauritano-Sahraoui Agreement, signed at Algiers, 10 August 1979, UN Docs A/34/427 and S/13503 (20 August 1979) at Annex I: <https://peacemaker.un.org/sites/peacemaker.un.org/files/MR_790810_Mauretanio-SahraouiAgreement.pdf> accessed 31 August 2023.

67 UNGA Res 34/37 (21 November 1979), para 5.

68 See ibid.; and UNGA Res 35/19 (11 November 1980), para 3.

69 UNGA Res 34/37 (21 November 1979), para 7; UNGA Res 35/19 (11 November 1980), para 10; and UNGA Res 36/46 (24 November 1981), para 6. But even though the General Assembly acknowledges the Polisario's privileged position in this regard, it has never been prepared to confer the status of 'national liberation movement' on the Polisario in a similar manner to the way it did for the PLO and SWAPO.

70 See Hodges (n 44) 279–306.

71 UNGA Res 34/37(1979), para 6 and UNGA Res 35/19 (1980), para 9.

to enter into direct negotiations with a view to ending their conflict.[72] The prospect of a negotiated solution grew after 1981, once the OAU became fully involved and the General Assembly threw its weight behind the idea of a regional solution to the conflict.

However, this breakthrough had a clear impact on the tone of the General Assembly's next resolution on Western Sahara. Resolution 36/46 (1981) welcomed the efforts of the OAU's Assembly of Heads of State and Governments, and the OAU's newly formed Implementation Committee on Western Sahara, to organise a democratic referendum through which the people of Western Sahara could exercise their right to self-determination.[73] The General Assembly again called on the Polisario and Morocco to enter into direct negotiations with one another and to conclude a peace treaty, which would facilitate the holding of a referendum regarding the Territory's final status.[74] At this point the OAU seized the initiative. In July 1978, Resolution AHG/Res.92(XV) was adopted at the 15th Ordinary Session of the OAU's Assembly of Heads of State and Government. It created an Ad Hoc Committee tasked with finding a solution to the Western Sahara Question which was compatible with the exercise of the right to self-determination. The Committee subsequently recommended that the Territory's people should be allowed to exercise their entitlement through the holding of a free and democratic referendum organised under the auspices of the UN and OAU. This position was endorsed in AHG/Res. 103(XVIII) during the OAU Assembly's 16th Ordinary Session in July 1979, and an Implementation Committee was established to consider the necessary arrangements for holding a proposed referendum.[75] In 1981, King Hassan II of Morocco conceded the idea of holding a referendum. However, Morocco's continuing resistance to this Committee's detailed proposals for a referendum resulted in the OAU's controversial 1984 decision to confer membership on the Sahrawi Arab Democratic Republic (SADR), a decision that led to Morocco's withdrawal from the Organisation.[76]

A pivotal development in the conflict occurred with Morocco's phased construction of a sand berm throughout the 1980s, which effectively partitioned the Territory to its advantage. The berm constitutes a substantial, fortified barrier running in a broadly diagonal direction for approximately 2,700 km across the length of Western Sahara. The sector to its west is controlled by Morocco and covers about 80% of the entire Territory while the eastern sector is a sparsely inhabited desert area controlled by the Polisario. The building of the berm did not herald victory for the Moroccan army, but it severely curtailed the Polisario's hitherto successful guerrilla warfare, resulting in a

72 UNGA Res 35/19 (1980), para 10.
73 UNGA Res 36/46 (24 November 1981), paras 1–4.
74 ibid., paras 5 and 6.
75 See Naldi (n 21) 17.
76 ibid., 18.

stalemate. This situation rendered the protagonists receptive to a negotiated solution.

(iii) Overview of the UN's Subsequent Involvement in the Western Sahara Question

Together the Security Council and the OAU brokered the 1988 Settlement Proposals by which Morocco and the Polisario agreed to a ceasefire and the holding of a referendum of the Territory's inhabitants, to be organised by the UN, with the electorate being determined by the census conducted by Spain in 1974.[77] During this period, both Morocco and the Polisario were acutely aware that if a multi-option referendum were to be held, the Territory's inhabitants would vote decisively in favour of independence.[78] Consequently, despite having agreed in principle to the holding of a referendum, the parties subsequently disputed the extent of the franchise and Morocco proved to be particularly implacable in this regard.[79] After several unsuccessful UN-sponsored initiatives to find a just, lasting, and mutually acceptable political solution to

77 The UN Security Council took note of the Settlement Proposals in Resolution 621 (20 September 1988) and it adopted the Secretary-General's Implementation Plan for Western Sahara via SCR 658, (27 June 1990), which sought to operationalise the 1988 Proposals. See the Secretary-General's Report on the situation in Western Sahara, UN Doc. S/21360, 18 June 1990. The Security Council endeavoured to facilitate this peace process by creating the UN Mission for the Referendum in Western Sahara (MINURSO): SCR 690, 29 April 1991. The OAU's involvement in the resolution of the Western Sahara Question diminished for some time thereafter, although it played an important role in negotiating the Settlement Proposals, which were agreed between the Polisario and Morocco in 1988. According to Naldi (n 21) 18, the OAU chose to adopt 'a policy of studied indifference' to the dispute after Morocco withdrew from the Organisation. Morocco was readmitted to the African Union in 2017 and the African Union has made serious attempts to engage with the situation in Western Sahara in recent years, despite Morocco's resistance to its involvement. See, the AU's 2015 Opinion on the Exploitation of Resources in Western Sahara: Legal opinion on the legality in the context of international law of actions allegedly taken in the exploration and/or exploitation of renewable and non-renewable natural resources or any other economic activity in Western Sahara | African Union (au.int) (accessed 31 August 2023). Further, see the AU's Troika Initiative concerning Western Sahara and its 2018 Nouakchott decision. Recent reports by the UN Secretary-General have catalogued some of the steps taken by the AU in this regard. See the discussion of the African Court of Human and Peoples' Rights' recent judgment in the *Bernard Mornah* Case in Chapter II(D)(ii) below.

78 See the Visiting Mission's 1975 Report (n 25) 12–128.

79 Both sides appreciated that the 1974 Spanish census was incomplete. The tasks of voter identification and registration were complicated by the difficulty of establishing the limits of familial ties. See Shelley (n 58) 187–193; Jensen (n 44) 49–62; Thilo Marauhn, 'Sahara', (2010) *Max Planck Encyclopedia of Public International Law*, paras 30–34; Soroeta (n 45) 244–252; and Christine Chinkin, 'The Security Council and Statehood', in C. Chinkin and F. Baetens (eds), *Sovereignty, Statehood and State Responsibility: Essays in Honour of James Crawford* (CUP 2013) 155–171.

the conflict,[80] it became clear that the Western Sahara Question would not be resolved within the framework created by the Settlement Proposals and so a new way forward had to be found.

The Secretary-General understood that the Western Sahara Question had to be settled by recourse to the principle of self-determination as applied within the process of decolonisation. However, the political reality of the situation prevailing in Western Sahara could not be ignored. Morocco insisted that it had enjoyed sovereignty over Rio de Oro and Sakiet El Hamra since time immemorial and it was not prepared to relinquish its grip over the Territory. The Polisario, on the other hand, continued to demand the holding of a referendum for the purpose of implementing the right to self-determination, despite having already unilaterally declared the SADR's existence by reference to this entitlement. The Secretary-General took the view that the parties would need to find a compromise between international legality and political reality and that this could only be achieved through direct negotiations.[81] Consequently, in 2007, at the Secretary-General's suggestion, the Security Council chose to adopt a *tabula rasa* approach, which was intended to shift the primary responsibility for finding a political solution to the parties themselves. It therefore decided to facilitate direct negotiations between Morocco and the Polisario to be conducted in good faith and without preconditions. However, the aim remained the same, namely: 'to achiev[e] a just, lasting and mutually acceptable political solution, which will provide for the self-determination of the people of Western Sahara in the context of arrangements consistent with the principles and purposes of the Charter of the United Nations'.[82]

Pursuant to the Security Council's new approach, Morocco submitted its autonomy plan to the Council on 11 April 2007. It proposed to exercise sovereignty over Western Sahara while putting autonomous arrangements in place to enable the Territory's inhabitants to manage their own internal affairs.[83] The idea that autonomous arrangements could be devised for Western Sahara was an interim feature of the rejected Baker peace plans of 2001 and 2003, but Morocco's plan envisaged the granting of autonomy as a permanent solution

80 See the UN Secretary-General's 2001 Report on the situation in Western Sahara (S/2001/613), Annex I regarding the first version of the Framework Agreement (the First Baker Plan). The Security Council supported a revised version (the Second Baker Plan) via SCR 1495 (31 July 2003). However, it was firmly rejected by Morocco on the ground that it did not respect Morocco's territorial integrity. See the Secretary-General's 2003 Report on the situation in Western Sahara, (S/2003/565), paras 50–55.

81 See the Secretary-General's Report on Western Sahara (2006/249), para 34.

82 SCR 1754 (30 April 2007), Preamble.

83 The Polisario's competing proposal, which was submitted to the Security Council on 10 April 2007, was grounded in the orthodox view that, in cases of decolonisation, the exercise of the right to self-determination requires the holding of a referendum with the option of independence being on the ballot paper.

to the dispute.[84] Autonomous arrangements are widely perceived as a means by which self-determination can be achieved in a specific territorial setting;[85] however, they are closely associated with the delivery of internal self-determination rather than with the right's external variant which is invariably engaged in instances of decolonisation. The negotiation and success of such governmental structures are heavily dependent on the existence of (hitherto absent) political will and trust between the parties, as well as the devising of intricate constitutional provisions and procedures.

The Security Council has taken note of Morocco's autonomy plan in the preamble to all its resolutions on Western Sahara since 2007, while 'welcoming serious and credible Moroccan efforts to move the process forward towards resolution'.[86] Consequently, third States have widely supposed that the Council views Morocco's plan as serious and credible.[87] Any autonomy arrangements tabled for discussion would be predicated on the assumption that Morocco already exercises sovereignty over Western Sahara as a matter of international law. However, this standpoint is fundamentally at odds with the approach endorsed by the UN and the African Union (AU).[88] For the UN, Western Sahara remains a NSGT and the exercise of the right to self-determination by the people concerned is still pending. As a result, Western Sahara's final status has not yet been definitively settled. The AU's position on the Western Sahara Question is apparent from the African Court of Human and Peoples' Rights judgment in the *Bernard Mornah* Case.[89] In the words of the Court, the AU and the UN 'recognise the situation of SADR as one of occupation and consider its territory as one of those territories whose decolonisation process is not yet fully complete'.[90] The UN and the AU may have conceptualised the situation in Western Sahara in materially different ways, but they both subscribe to the same viewpoint – Morocco does not currently exercise sovereignty over Western Sahara/SADR as a matter of international law.[91]

84 See Baker Plans above (n 80).

85 See Zelim Skurbaty (ed), *Beyond a One-Dimensional State: An Emerging Right to Autonomy?* (Martinus Nijhoff 2005); Markku Suksi (ed), *Autonomy: Applications and Implications* (Kluwer Law International 1998); and Hurst Hannum, *Autonomy, Sovereignty and Self-Determination: The Accommodation of Conflicting Rights* (University of Pennsylvania Press 1990).

86 See SCR 1754 (30 April 2007) and see discussion in Chapter V(A) below. In contrast, the Security Council only took note of the Polisario's proposal, submitted to the Council on 10 April 2007.

87 See discussion in Chapter V(A) below.

88 Both the SADR and Morocco are AU member States. The OAU, the AU's predecessor, admitted the SADR to membership of the Organisation in 1982 with Morocco withdrawing in protest in 1984 when the SADR took up its seat. See Naldi (n 21). Morocco joined the AU in 2017.

89 Judgment of the African Court of Human and Peoples' Rights in *Bernard Mornah v Benin et al* (22 Sept 2022). Discussed in Chapter II(D)(ii) below.

90 *Bernard Mornah* Judgment, para 301.

91 This shared position also underpins the reasoning adopted by the ICJ in its *Western Sahara* Advisory Opinion and has been accepted by the CJEU in its judgments in Case C-104/16P *Council*

It is notable that the Security Council has never characterised Morocco's presence in Western Sahara as amounting to a military occupation.[92] Indeed, it has refrained from acknowledging that Morocco has committed any violations of international law arising from its conduct in the Territory.[93] Further, neither the Security Council nor the General Assembly has called upon third States and IOs to withhold recognition of Morocco's assertion of sovereignty and to refrain from dealing with it in relation to Western Sahara. The USA, the Council's penholder on the Western Sahara file, and France have consistently supported Morocco's autonomy proposal for many years.[94] In 2018, the Council introduced significant changes to the content of its resolutions on Western Sahara thereby signalling a shift away from its established formula, which focused predominantly on delivering self-determination for the people of Western Sahara, in favour of promoting the need for pragmatism and realism in the search for a political solution.[95] Such an emphasis on realpolitik considerations indicates that the Council views the territorial status quo as representing the baseline for negotiations rather than seeing the principles and mechanisms of decolonisation as providing the main frame of reference. The Council's apparent acceptance of the credibility of Morocco's autonomy plan confers a degree of legitimacy on those States which condone Morocco's sovereignty claim because it allows them to express their support for this UN-facilitated peace process while adopting a position that is at odds with established international legality as far as the Western Sahara Question is concerned.[96]

Despite the General Assembly's historical commitment to ensuring the exercise of the right to self-determination by the Territory's inhabitants via the holding of a referendum, in recent times, its resolutions on the Western Sahara Question have become more abstract, qualified, and conciliatory in nature.[97] In addition, there has been growing support for Morocco's autonomy plan and its sovereignty claim to Western Sahara among States participating in the General Assembly's committees during the last few years, even though

v Front Polisario [2016] EU:C:2016:973; and Case C-266/16 R *(Western Sahara Campaign UK) v HMRC & Secretary of State for the Environment* [2018] EU:C:2018:18. These cases are discussed below.

92 See Martin Dawidowicz, 'Trading Fish or Human Rights in Western Sahara' in Duncan French (ed), *Statehood and Self-Determination* (CUP 2013) 250–276, 272–273.

93 T Ruys, 'The Role of State Immunity and Act of State in the NM Cherry Blossom Case and the Western Sahara Dispute' (2019) 68 *ICLQ* 67, 85.

94 See Chapters IV and V below.

95 See SCR 2414 (2018), SCR 2440 (2018), SCR 2468 (2019) and 2548 (2020), 2602 (2021) and 2654 (2022).

96 See statements made in the C24 and Fourth Committee, as discussed in Chapter IV(B)(i) below.

97 See Chapter IV(B) below.

this significant shift is not currently reflected in the Assembly's latest resolutions on this issue.[98]

In his 2021 Report on Western Sahara, the Secretary-General observed that the situation in the Territory had 'significantly deteriorated', resulting in the resumption of hostilities between Morocco and the Polisario.[99] In late October 2020, a group of Sahrawi civilian protesters entered the demilitarised buffer strip near the border town of Guerguerat in Western Sahara for the purpose of making peaceful demands about the Western Sahara conflict, thereby blocking traffic on this arterial route into neighbouring Mauritania.[100] An armed Polisario military detachment was then deployed in the buffer strip to protect the civilian group, in violation of Military Agreement No. 1.[101] In early November 2020, Morocco mobilised and stationed a significant military force nearby, also in breach of this Agreement.[102] On 13 November 2020, officials of the UN Mission for the Referendum in Western Sahara (MINURSO) observed civilians leaving the buffer strip and firing incidents between the Polisario and Moroccan forces in that area. The Moroccan army subsequently entered the buffer strip and began to construct a new section of the sand berm in this prohibited zone.[103] In response, the Polisario declared an end to the ceasefire and the resumption of hostilities.[104] The UN Secretary-General referred in 2021 to the continuing low-intensity conflict.[105] He observed that the 'status of the buffer strip as a demilitarised zone remains a cornerstone of a peaceful solution' to the dispute.[106] He also lamented the 'daily incursions into this zone' and the resumption of hostilities while saying that this amounted to a 'major setback' which could entail a further escalation to the conflict.[107]

In his 2022 Western Sahara Report, the Secretary-General provided an update regarding the ongoing hostilities between the protagonists, including an account of reported firing incidents involving both sides, drone strikes conducted by the Moroccan army in the Territory, along with some information concerning casualties and damage caused.[108] These instances seem to have

98 Notably, in the C24 and Fourth Committee. Recent developments in the Security Council and General Assembly concerning the Western Sahara Question and their significance in the context of the right to self-determination and the doctrine of recognition are discussed in Chapter IV below.

99 See the Secretary-General's Report on the Situation in Western Sahara, S/2021/843 (1 October 2021) para 2.

100 ibid., paras 3–4. The Polisario has long maintained that Morocco violated the ceasefire agreement by building a road through the buffer strip.

101 ibid., para 8.

102 ibid., para 10.

103 ibid., para 13.

104 ibid., para 15.

105 ibid., para 16.

106 ibid., para 84.

107 ibid.

108 Secretary-General's Report, S/2022/733 (3 October 2022), paras 2–18.

followed a similar pattern to those reported in the previous year prompting the Secretary-General to repeat his earlier assessment of the situation.[109] He concluded that such negative developments had produced 'a fundamentally changed operational and political environment' for MINURSO, especially to the east of the berm.[110] Nevertheless, several States have taken the view that Morocco's response to the Guerguerat crisis amounted to legitimate action taken by a sovereign State to protect its citizens and to maintain free movement across its national territory.[111] The resumption of hostilities appears to represent a pivotal moment in the dispute as far as third States supportive of Morocco's cause are concerned. It has not only marked an increasing willingness on the part of certain States to voice their support for Morocco's claim to Western Sahara but also to adopt concrete measures in this regard, as demonstrated by the spate of consulates which have been established in Western Sahara, especially since 2020.[112]

The outstanding challenge posed by the Western Sahara Question remains how to settle a frustrated case of decolonisation, concerning a NSGT, in a way that would uphold the principle of self-determination without following the established modalities associated with that process. This task has been made more difficult by jurisprudential developments which have strengthened the normative resonance of the right to self-determination since the *Western Sahara* Advisory Opinion was delivered. It is now indisputable that this entitlement generates *erga omnes* obligations and, although the ICJ has been reluctant to affirm this directly, the right is widely considered to have acquired the status of a peremptory norm of international law.[113] The consequences of this entitlement for third States and IOs have evolved significantly as a result.

The protracted Western Sahara dispute is exceptional in many ways. However, it is suggested that this hard case reveals much about the content and operation of the doctrines of self-determination and recognition more generally, and it may give pause for thought regarding the communitarian impulses that are presumed to underpin contemporary international law.

109 ibid., para 89.

110 ibid., paras 9, 94, 101.

111 See e.g., the statements made by the following States in the 2021 meetings of the C24 dedicated to the Western Sahara Question: Ivory Coast (C24, 2021, 2nd meeting, para 89), Grenada, (3rd meeting, para 13), Saudi Arabia (3rd meeting, para 26), Bahrain (3rd meeting, para 44), Gabon (3rd meeting, para 48), Senegal (3rd meeting, para 52) and the Comoros (3rd meeting, para 55). See Chapter IV(B)(i) below.

112 See the discussion in Chapter V(B) below.

113 See e.g., *East Timor (Portugal v Australia) Case* (Judgment) [1995] ICJ Rep 102, para 29; *Legal Consequences of the Construction of a Wall in the Occupied Palestinian Territory* (Advisory Opinion) [2004] ICJ Rep 136, para 159; *Legal Consequences of the Separation of the Chagos Archipelago from Mauritius in 1965* (Advisory Opinion) [2019] ICJ Rep 95, para 180; the *Bernard Mornah* Case, para 298 (where the African Court of Human and Peoples' Rights affirms that the right is *jus cogens*).

B. The SADR's Struggle for Recognition as a State

In the broadest possible sense, recognition is – as Shaw puts it – 'a method of accepting certain factual situations and endowing them with legal significance'.[114] Recognition of statehood, and its withdrawal, are political acts, although they have significant international legal effects.[115] Article 6 of the Montevideo Convention describes recognition as 'unconditional and irrevocable', but general international law does not prevent States from revoking recognition or attaching conditions to an act of recognition.[116]

While it is true to say that withdrawal of recognition 'is not a very general occurrence',[117] the practice relating to the SADR is idiosyncratic. Of the 83 States that have recognised the SADR since its existence was proclaimed by the Polisario Front in 1976, 39 have 'withdrawn', 'frozen', or 'suspended' recognition since the 1990s.[118]

This extraordinary practice is the fruit of intensive diplomatic efforts by Morocco, pursued while consolidating its military control over most of the territory of Western Sahara. Grant views the Moroccan strategy as similar to the 'Hallstein doctrine' deployed by West Germany in the 1950s – an attempt 'to enforce and generalize against East Germany a unilateral regime of non-recognition'.[119] He observes that, after Morocco withdrew from the OAU in 1984 in protest against the SADR's admission, 'it applied the Hallstein doctrine to multilateral organizations as well as states; recognition of the SADR by either type of entity … was to be met with severance of relations'.[120]

114 Malcolm Shaw, *International Law* (9th ed, CUP 2021) 189.

115 James Crawford, *Creation of States* (2nd ed, OUP 2006) 27: 'Recognition is an institution of State practice that can resolve uncertainties as to status and allow for new situations to be regularized'.

116 The Montevideo 'Convention on the Rights and Duties of States' (1933), 165 *LNTS* 19, has only 17 parties.

117 Shaw (n 114) 397. Shaw gives the example of the 1940 withdrawal of recognition by the UK of the Italian conquest of Ethiopia, which it had recognised *de facto* in 1936 and *de jure* two years later.

118 The Wikipedia page, 'International recognition of the Sahrawi Arab Democratic Republic', contains an impressive, referenced, compendium of the practice: <https://en.wikipedia.org/wiki/International_recognition_of_the_Sahrawi_Arab_Democratic_Republic> accessed 31 August 2023. The authors are indebted to the individuals who have compiled the valuable information on this page.

119 Thomas D Grant, 'Hallstein Revisited: Unilateral Enforcement of Regimes of Non-Recognition Since the Two Germanies' (2000) 36 *StanJIntl L* 221, 222, and 233–236 (for a discussion of Morocco and the SADR).

120 ibid., 234. Grant remains cautious regarding the effectiveness of the doctrine in the case of the SADR, saying that 'other factors, such as pressure of influential aid donor states, such as France, and Moroccan military success in the Western Sahara theater may have contributed, as much as did the Hallstein-like exercise, to a shift in recognition policy against the SADR' (236).

Grant was writing in 2000, but the strategy he describes continues to be pursued relentlessly by Morocco. As King Mohammed VI put it on 21 August 2022, 'I would like to send a clear message to the world: the Sahara issue is the prism through which Morocco views its international environment'.[121] Five days after the King had made those remarks, Morocco recalled its ambassador to Tunisia, an otherwise friendly regional neighbour, after Tunisia had invited the President of the SADR to an African development summit.[122]

The story of how this point was reached can broadly be divided into two phases. The first phase consists of a slew of recognitions from States, from the time of the proclamation of the SADR in 1976 to the end of the Cold War. During the second phase – from the 1990s to the present day – around half of the States that had previously recognised the SADR said they were withdrawing, suspending, or 'freezing' their recognition, with few new recognitions to counterbalance this trend (although, as will be seen, there have been several renewals of recognition by States that had previously purported to withdraw, suspend, or freeze recognition).[123]

An exhaustive analysis of this practice is beyond the scope of this book, but it is instructive to look at the reasoning of certain States when changing their policy on the recognition of the SADR. For instance, it is worth considering the approaches of the States that rushed to recognise the SADR in the immediate aftermath of its proclamation of independence on 27 February 1976, in chronological order: Madagascar (28 February 1976), Burundi (1 March 1976), Algeria (6 March 1976), Angola and Benin (11 March 1976), Mozambique (13 March 1976), Guinea-Bissau (15 March 1976) North Korea (16 March 1976), Togo (17 March 1976), and Rwanda (1 April 1976). Of these States, half – Madagascar, Benin, Burundi, Guinea-Bissau, and Togo – have since changed their position, sometimes more than once. A brief survey of some of the reasons given publicly for these changes in policy provides useful insight into the types of forces that are at work.

Madagascar purported to 'freeze' ('*geler*') its recognition of the SADR on 6 April 2005, after forming closer relations with Morocco.[124] Both the statements of the Moroccan and the Madagascan governments in respect of this change of policy underscored the importance of UN involvement on the path towards a political solution. Madagascar, for its part, assured the Moroccan

121 Security Council Report, 'Africa: Western Sahara' (October 2022), <https://www.securitycouncilreport.org/monthly-forecast/2022-10/western-sahara-9.php> accessed 31 August 2023

122 ibid. See also, 'Morocco Recalls Tunisia Ambassador Over Western Sahara' *Al-Jazeera* (27 August 2022), <https://www.aljazeera.com/news/2022/8/27/morocco-recalls-tunisia-ambassador-over-western-sahara> accessed 31 August 2023.

123 See generally <https://en.wikipedia.org/wiki/International_recognition_of_the_Sahrawi_Arab_Democratic_Republic> accessed 31 August 2023

124 'Madagascar gèle sa reconnaissance de la "RASD"', 6 April 2005, <http://www.yabiladi.com/forum/madagascar-gele-reconnaissance-rasd-2-540000.html> accessed 31 August 2023.

King of its determination, in an 'engaged, sincere and neutral' manner, to support the efforts of the UN in achieving a political solution in accordance with the wishes of the international community.[125]

Benin 'cancelled' its recognition of the SADR on 21 March 1997.[126] The Ambassador of Benin to the Kingdom of Morocco said in 2015 that his country's original 'principled' support for the Polisario was a product of Cold War politics, and of Benin's decision to champion causes it considered 'progressive'. He referred to 1990 and the collapse of the Berlin Wall as a turning point in Benin's approach to the issue. Expressing concerns about the violence in Mali and surrounding States, he said that an independent Western Sahara could become a haven for terrorists and result in 'balkanisation'. For this reason, he opposed independence as 'unrealistic', and took the view that Morocco's plan for a 'large' degree of autonomy for the territory was 'credible and serious'.[127]

Burundi froze its recognition of the SADR on 5 May 2006, lifted the freeze on 16 June 2008, and most recently cancelled its recognition outright on 25 October 2010.[128] Its swift reversal two years after the initial 'freeze' was motivated by a desire to move towards a common foreign policy for the East African Community, and its decision to withdraw recognition was taken ostensibly 'to encourage, like many other countries, the UN process and the momentum brought about by the Moroccan autonomy initiative'.[129]

Having recognised the SADR in 1976, Guinea-Bissau withdrew its recognition on 2 April 1997, re-recognised the SADR on 26 May 2009, and

125 ibid.

126 Interview with Ambassador of Benin, Bio Toro Orou Guiwa, *La Voix du Centre*, 2 May 2015, <https://web.archive.org/web/20150502071445/http://lvc.ma/index.php/interviews/item/152-m-bio-toro-orou-guiwa-ambassadeur-du-benin> accessed 31 August 2023.

127 ibid.

128 'Burundi freezes recognition of so-called Sahrawi republic', Maghreb Arab Press, 10 May 2006, <https://web.archive.org/web/20060520082428/http://www.map.ma/eng/sections/politics/burundi_freezes_reco/view> accessed 31 August 2023); a copy of the Note Verbale of 16 June 2008 reversing/'lifting' the freezing decision ('lever … le gel' in French, literally 'lift the freeze') is available at: <http://saharaoccidental.blogspot.com/2008/06/burundi.html> accessed 31 August 2023. A joint statement said that Burundi had eventually taken the decision to withdraw recognition 'to encourage, like many other countries, the UN process and the momentum brought about by the Moroccan autonomy initiative', with the Burundian minister 'express[ing] his intention to support the efforts made under the auspices of the UN by the Secretary-General and his Personal Envoy to reach a final, mutually acceptable political solution to this regional dispute', and both parties agreeing 'to strengthen the political dialogue between the two countries and to give fresh momentum to bilateral relations, especially in the economic and technical field for the benefit of both brotherly peoples'. 'Burundi withdraws recognition of "SADR"', *Maghreb Arab Presse*, 25 October 2010, <https://web.archive.org/web/20101027183913/http://www.map.ma/eng/sections/politics/burundi_withdraws_re/view> accessed 31 August 2023.

129 ibid.

withdrew its recognition again on 30 March 2010.[130] Following this latest withdrawal of recognition, a Minister of State and presidential adviser of Guinea-Bissau signalled his country's support for the Moroccan autonomy plan. He struck a pragmatic tone, saying that Morocco had always been by Guinea-Bissau's side since its war of independence, and he expressed hopes of strengthening the economic relationship between the two countries, especially in the light of the difficult economic situation in which Guinea-Bissau found itself. Mention was also made of the fact that, the previous December, the President of Guinea-Bissau had been treated in a Moroccan hospital after he was shot by a member of his security team.

Also of interest is the phenomenon of groups of Caribbean and Pacific Island States withdrawing recognition of the SADR *en masse* and throwing their collective weight behind the Moroccan autonomy plan. Grenada, Antigua and Barbuda, Saint Kitts and Nevis, and Saint Lucia announced their withdrawal of recognition of the SADR in joint statements following visits by the Moroccan Foreign Minister on 9–13 August 2021.[131] Another significant development was the adoption of the Laayoune Declaration at the Third Morocco–Pacific Island States Forum, on 26 February 2020.[132] The signatories to this Declaration were Fiji, Kiribati, Marshall Islands, Micronesia, Nauru, Palau, Papua New Guinea, Samoa, Solomon Islands, Tonga, Tuvalu, and Vanuatu. The Declaration focuses on the development of mutual co-operation between Morocco and the participating Pacific Island States in a wide range of areas, including the need for concerted action to tackle the adverse effects of climate change; education and vocational training; agriculture, fisheries, health, and tourism as well as broader shared goals of international peace and security and sustainable development. However, it is notable that the planned co-operative measures and assistance were tied to Morocco's recognition strategy concerning Western Sahara. Specifically, in paragraph 12 of the Laayoune Declaration, the signatories:

> solemnly affirm that the Sahara region is an integral part of Moroccan territory, and consider that the Moroccan Autonomy Initiative is the only

130 The Government of Guinea-Bissau talks of putting an end to recognition and backing the autonomy initiative, while hoping to strengthen economic relations with Morocco: 'Guinea Bissau retira su reconocimiento a la RASD y apoya iniciativa autonomía', *ADN*, 30 March 2010, <https://web.archive.org/web/20110719235533/http://www.adn.es/internacional/20100330/NWS-2715-RASD-Bissau-Guinea-reconocimiento-iniciativa.html> accessed 31 August 2023.

131 Statement by Moroccan Ministry of Foreign Affairs, 16 August 2010, <https://web.archive.org/web/20140116193414/http://www.diplomatie.ma/articledetails.aspx?id=5549> accessed 31 August 2023.

132 The Laayoune Declaration, adopted 26 February 2020 during the third Morocco–Pacific Island States Forum <https://www.diplomatie.ma/en/3rd-morocco-pacific-island-states-forum-morocco-and-nauru-sign-several-cooperation-agreements-laayoune> accessed 31 August 2023.

> and unique solution to the regional dispute on the Moroccan Sahara. We support the efforts led under the exclusive aegis of the United Nations towards achieving a realistic, practicable, and enduring solution to this regional dispute in full respect of Morocco's territorial integrity and national sovereignty.

The small sample of cases discussed above provides a representative insight into the range of motivations and rationalisations being advanced by States when changing their recognition policy. There is a spectrum of ostensible reasons, from the principled (focusing on the need for a multilateral solution overseen by the UN, and concerns for regional stability), to the pragmatic (with appeals to 'realism' and the practical likelihood of securing a peaceful outcome), to more basic material calculations (economic interests and post–Cold War allegiances).[133] What is noticeably absent from these statements is any concern for the right of the Sahrawi people to determine their own future, or any sense that endorsing the Moroccan occupation could be an affront to the international rules on self-determination and territorial integrity, with possible consequences for other cases and for the stability of the international system as a whole.

Perhaps the most poignant example of the interplay between basic self-interest and lofty principles is the approach of Mauritius, which withdrew its recognition of the SADR on 16 January 2014 but promptly resumed its recognition on 23 November 2015. The renewed recognition came eight months after Mauritius' success in a UN Convention on the Law of the Sea (UNCLOS) Annex VII arbitration against the UK, concerning the designation by the UK of a marine protected area around the Chagos Archipelago.[134] With one eye on its plan to bring the Chagos question before the ICJ – a question eventually (and carefully) framed as a decolonisation matter rather than as a bilateral dispute – Mauritius announced that 'recognition of the SADR as a sovereign and independent State is a reaffirmation of the support of Mauritius for the Western Sahara people's inalienable right to self-determination'.[135]

133 A Sahrawi official, referring to the fact that in the five years to 2021, the number of Latin American embassies in Rabat had increased from 5 to 12, opined that this was the result of the 'politics of the cheque book': <https://elpais.com/internacional/2021-04-22/marruecos-gana-terreno-en-latinoamerica-en-su-batalla-por-el-sahara-occidental.html> accessed 31 August 2023.

134 Chagos Marine Protected Area (Mauritius v. United Kingdom), Annex VII Tribunal, Award, 18 March 2015.

135 According to the Mauritian government, 'The cabinet has agreed to Mauritius recognizing anew the Saharawi Arab Democratic Republic (SADR) as a sovereign State, in line with the aim of the Government to forge new relationships across the world as enunciated in the Government Programme 2015-2019', SADR Mission to the AU press release, 23 November 2015, <https://web.archive.org/web/20151126061044/http://www.sadr-emb-au.net/mauritius-re-establishes-diplomatic-relations-with-sadr/> accessed 31 August 2023.

It is interesting to note that, even when it initially withdrew its recognition of the SADR in 2014, Mauritius had attempted to couch its justification in the language of principled multilateralism, expressing 'its determination to continue supporting efforts by the UN seeking to find a just, equitable solution that is acceptable by all the parties to the conflict over the Sahara'.[136] As Mauritius has subsequently discovered to its advantage, there is more appetite within the General Assembly for upholding the principles of self-determination and territorial integrity when the State in unlawful occupation of territory awaiting decolonisation is the UK.

136 Moroccan Government press release, 15 January 2014, <https://www.maroc.ma/en/news/republic-mauritius-withdraws-recognition-so-called-sadr> accessed 31 August 2023.

3 The Doctrine of Recognition and Morocco's Claim to Western Sahara

A. The Duty of Non-Recognition

The granting (or withholding) of recognition is generally acknowledged to be a discretionary act except for instances where third States and International Organisations (IOs) are bound by a legal duty of non-recognition.[1] The doctrine of recognition is available to States and IOs in situations involving the creation of a new State, government, or a novel territorial claim made by an existing State. The collective obligation of non-recognition may arise in a situation forged or maintained through the violation of a peremptory norm of general international law by the wrongdoing State (or territorial entity) in question. As Orakhelashvili puts it:

> [T]he duty of non-recognition of the breaches of peremptory norms extends not only to State-creation but to every kind of illegality. It refers to the general duty to refrain from acts and actions, or from taking attitudes, that imply the recognition of the acts offending peremptory norms in a variety of international legal relations.[2]

That being said, discussions concerning the doctrine of non-recognition often revolve around the acquisition of territory by force and the legal validity of new territorial arrangements.[3]

The duty of non-recognition finds its normative origins in the principle of *ex injuria jus non oritur*, but it is widely believed to have acquired the status of customary international law and an *erga omnes* character.[4] The duty's

1 The character of the doctrine of recognition is discussed in Sections (B) and (C) below.

2 Alexander Orakhelashvili, *Peremptory Norms in International Law* (OUP 2006) 282.

3 James Crawford, *State Responsibility: The General Part* (CUP 2013) 382: 'The archetypal example of the operation of non-recognition is that of territorial acquisition resulting from aggression'.

4 See Hersch Lauterpacht, *Recognition in International Law* (1947, CUP 2013 reprint) 420; Stefan Talmon, 'The Duty Not to "Recognise as Lawful" a Situation Created by the Illegal Use of Force or Other Serious Breaches of a Jus Cogens Obligation: An Obligation without Real Substance?' in Christian Tomuschat and Jean-Marc Thouvenin (eds), *The Fundamental Rules of the*

DOI: 10.4324/9781032658827-3

contemporary scope and content were enumerated in Chapter 3 of the Articles on the Responsibility of States for Internationally Wrongful Acts (ARSIWA). Article 40(1) specified that: 'This Chapter applies to the international responsibility which is entailed by a serious breach by a State of an obligation arising under a peremptory norm of general international law'.[5] Confirmed examples include the prohibition on the threat or use of force vis-à-vis territorial annexation and the denial of the right to self-determination.[6] Article 41 identified the consequences flowing from the violation of such norms, namely:

1. States shall co-operate to bring to an end through lawful means any serious breach within the meaning of article 40.
2. No State shall recognise as lawful a situation created by a serious breach within the meaning of article 40, nor render aid or assistance in maintaining that situation.[7]

Notwithstanding these provisions, the International Law Commission did not explain how a duty of non-recognition could be triggered in the ARSIWA or its accompanying Commentary. Consequently, it is unclear whether prior institutional approval is required – and if so, which body is competent to impose such a collective obligation – or whether its emergence remains a matter for individual States and IOs to determine for themselves by reference to the applicable law.

It is indisputable that a duty of non-recognition may be declared by the Security Council, pursuant to the exercise of its Chapter 7 powers, and such a decision will be legally binding on member States and IOs by the coincidence of Articles 25 and 41 of the United Nations (UN) Charter. However, the Council has rarely invoked its Chapter 7 powers in the context of declaring a duty of non-recognition in response to illegal situations arising from the grave violation of international law.[8] Moreover, in its *Namibia* Advisory Opinion, the International Court of Justice (ICJ) ruled that the Council's capacity to render binding decisions, pursuant to Article 25, was not restricted to the exercise of the enforcement power contained in Chapter 7.[9] In practice, the

International Legal Order: Jus Cogens and Obligations Erga Omnes (Brill 2005) 99, 113; and John Dugard, *The Secession of States and Their Recognition in the Wake of Kosovo* (The Hague Academy, 2013) 82.

5 In Crawford's view (n 3) 381, 'the mere fact of breach [of a *jus cogens* norm] is ordinarily sufficient to warrant the label of "serious"'.

6 See James Crawford, *The International Law Commission's Articles on State Responsibility: Introduction, Text and Commentaries* (CUP 2002) 245–47, paras 1–5.

7 Also see Articles 41 and 42(2) DARIO.

8 See Talmon (n 4) 112–113.

9 See *Legal Consequences for States of the Continued Presence of South Africa in Namibia (South West Africa) notwithstanding Security Council Resolution 276 (1970)* (Advisory Opinion) [1971] *ICJ Rep* 31, paras 113–115.

Council has largely called upon States to refrain from recognising particular illegal situations by reference to Chapter VI of the UN Charter and it has often used hortatory and/or relatively sparse language in such resolutions.[10] This modus operandi may indicate that the Council's resolutions do not manifest a legally binding character unless its Chapter VII powers are being invoked. However, in the *Namibia* Advisory Opinion, the ICJ made it clear that the use of exhortative language is not necessarily a barrier to the making of a binding Council decision. Specifically, the Court observed that: 'The language of a resolution of the Security Council should be carefully analysed before a conclusion can be made as to its binding effect' along with all the circumstances that might assist in determining its legal consequences.[11]

It has been argued that the duty of non-recognition derives its binding character directly from a concrete decision made by the Security Council within the ambit of its Charter powers, which is then legally binding on States and IOs on a collective basis.[12] On this reasoning, unless and until the Council has declared the existence of a collective duty of non-recognition in a concrete setting, third States and IOs are free to determine the scope, nature, and extent of their dealings with the target State (or entity) for themselves.[13] A clear advantage of requiring the prior approval of the Security Council (or the ICJ) is that it produces a high degree of certainty as far as third States and IOs are concerned and it is also of great value because such a decision provides clear authority for third parties to take appropriate countermeasures against the wrongdoer in an effort to prompt it to conform to its international

10 Talmon (n 4) 113; and Enrico Milano, 'The non-recognition of Russia's annexation of Crimea: three different legal approaches and one unanswered question' (2014) *QIL* 35–55, 50.

11 *Namibia* (Advisory Opinion), para 144. Some scholars may be tempted to argue that 'calling upon States' not to recognise this or that situation or regime is more in keeping with a request than an instruction giving rise to a legal obligation. However, on this point see Judge Weeramantry's reasoning in his Dissenting Opinion in the *East Timor* Case, at 205–208.

12 See Judge Higgins' Separate Opinion in the *Wall* Advisory Opinion (2004), para 38; Alison Pert, 'The "Duty" of Non-Recognition in Contemporary International Law: Issues and Uncertainties' Sydney Law School – Legal Studies Research Paper No 13/96 (December 2013) 12–13 <http://papers.ssrn.com/sol3/papers.cfm?abstract_id=2368618≥ accessed 31 August 2023; Milano (n 10) 47–48; and Talmon (n 4) 110. In its ARSIWA Commentary, the International Law Commission (ILC) relied extensively on cases where the Security Council had declared a duty of non-recognition . See Crawford (n 6) 250–251, paras 6–10.

13 The International Law Association's Committee on Recognition/Non-Recognition undertook a survey of State practice for its Second Report (Washington Conference, March 2014). The Committee found little cogent evidence in support of the existence of a general duty of non-recognition in the absence of a binding obligation being declared by, for example, the UN Security Council (pp. 3–7). However, it added that many States appear reluctant to confirm or deny the existence of a duty of non-recognition and such unwillingness may be attributable to considerations of political exigency (p. 5). See the position adopted by Australia in its Counter-Memorial in the East Timor proceedings, para 365: Pert (n 12) 14–15.

legal obligations in a particular situation.[14] A corollary of this approach is that the threshold is too high for the collective obligation to be triggered in all but the most extreme cases, limiting the practical relevance of the duty in international relations.

In contrast, many international lawyers have argued that the duty of non-recognition is triggered by the ordinary processes concerning the formation of customary international law.[15] The ICJ's efforts to elaborate the duty of non-recognition in its *Namibia* Advisory Opinion were undoubtedly influenced by its interpretation that Security Council Resolution 276 (1970) constituted a binding decision, notwithstanding the Court's view that the scope and operation of this obligation were also normatively underpinned by customary international law.[16] It ruled that the obligation to deny the *erga omnes* validity of South Africa's exercise of governmental authority in respect of Namibia was binding on member States and non-member States alike. If it had taken the view that the binding character of the Security Council's decisions flowed from the special significance of the UN Charter, pursuant to Article 103, it would be difficult to comprehend how such resolutions necessarily create binding international legal obligations for non-member States, despite the UN's objective legal personality.[17]

Proponents of the institutional approach are concerned about the prospect of a duty of non-recognition emerging in a concrete setting without an authoritative decision having been made by a competent body since this would result in the creation of an obligation that will bind all third States and IOs automatically. However, it is important to appreciate that any such potential obligation should be characterised as 'self-judging' or 'self-executing' as such situations engage the process of auto-interpretation rather than the creation of automatically binding obligations per se.[18] Individual States and IOs must decide for themselves whether the established requirements for triggering this duty have been met in each case and they may be held responsible for their decisions

14 See Article 22 ARSIWA and Martin Dawidowicz, *Third-Party Countermeasures in International Law* (CUP 2017).

15 See, e.g., Judge Skubiszewski's Dissenting Opinion in the *East Timor* Case, para 125. Also, see Lauterpacht, Talmon, and Dugard above (n 4).

16 Paragraph 2 of Security Council Resolution 276 (1970): 'Declare[d] the continuing presence of the South African authorities in Namibia is illegal and consequently all acts taken by the Government of South Africa on behalf of or concerning Namibia after the termination of the Mandate are illegal and invalid'. Paragraph 5 'Call[ed] upon all States, particularly those which have economic and other interests in Namibia, to refrain from any dealings with the Government of South Africa that are inconsistent with paragraph 2 of the present resolution'.

17 Tams argues that the ICJ harnessed the concept of *erga omnes* in the *Namibia* Advisory Opinion solely to ensure that the Security Council resolutions concerning the unlawful situation in Namibia were legally binding on States that were not UN members at that time. See Christian Tams, *Enforcing Obligation Erga Omnes in International Law* (CUP 2005) 107–109.

18 Antonio Cassese, *International Law* (2nd ed., 2005) 6.

in this regard.[19] Given the decentralised structure of the international legal order and the absence of an international court or tribunal endowed with general compulsory jurisdiction to render binding decisions, it is conceivable that individual States may adopt different, but plausible, interpretations of the applicable international law based on their reading of the available evidence.[20]

The ICJ reconsidered the significance of UN resolutions in the context of the obligations *erga omnes* associated with the right to self-determination and the duty of non-recognition in the *East Timor* Case.[21] Until Australia concluded the 1989 Timor Gap Treaty with Indonesia, no third State had formally recognised Indonesia's sovereignty claim to East Timor.[22] However, despite the adoption of two Security Council resolutions, pursuant to Chapter VI of the UN Charter, which were strongly critical of Indonesia's annexation of this Non-Self-Governing Territory (NSGT) through the use of force along with eight General Assembly resolutions condemning Indonesia's actions in this setting, the ICJ was not prepared to rule that a duty of non-recognition had arisen on the facts.[23] As the Court observed in this regard:

> Without prejudice to the question whether the resolutions under discussion could be binding in nature, [...] they cannot be regarded as 'givens' which constitute a sufficient basis for determining the dispute between the Parties.[24]

This position could be interpreted as supporting the proposition that a duty of non-recognition can only arise if there is explicit and cogent institutional support for such a collective obligation via an appropriately phrased Security Council resolution, or, more tentatively, a comparable General Assembly resolution.[25] However, in the *East Timor* Case, it is arguable that the ICJ embraced a more subtle position than might otherwise be supposed. Instead of treating UN resolutions as decisions to which it was bound to give effect, the Court indicated that they could constitute evidence from which a duty of non-recognition may be discerned in appropriate cases.[26] However, as Indonesia

19 See Milano (n 10) 49; Talmon (n 4) 113 and 122.

20 See Ian Brownlie, 'Recognition in Theory and Practice' (1982) 53 *BYIL* 197, 205.

21 *East Timor (Portugal v Australia) Case* [1995] *ICJ Rep* 102.

22 See James Crawford, *Chance, Order, Change: The Course of International Law* (The Hague Academy 2014) 52.

23 In particular, see GAR 31/53 (1 December 1976); SCR 389 (22 April 1976); and GAR 32/34 (13 December 1978).

24 East Timor Judgment (1995) para 34.

25 For a recent discussion of the significance of General Assembly resolutions in the context of the duty of non-recognition see: the *Coastal State Rights Case (Ukraine/Russia) Award on Preliminary Objections*, Annex VII Tribunal (16 March 2020) paras 170–177.

26 See Thomas Grant, 'East Timor, the U.N. System, and Enforcing Non-Recognition in International Law' (2000) 33 *VandJTransnatlL* 273, 309.

was deemed to be an indispensable third party to the proceedings, the ICJ was unable to evaluate such evidence to determine whether a duty of non-recognition existed because it had no jurisdiction to decide the case.[27]

Notwithstanding the significance of the jurisprudential debate canvassed above, even those international lawyers who deny that prior institutional approval is required to trigger the duty of non-recognition appreciate that co-ordinated institutional action is needed for this collective obligation to be rendered effective as far as third States and IOs are concerned.[28] Consequently, in practice, UN institutional approval is widely seen as crucial to the operational viability of any duty of non-recognition in concrete settings given its fundamental purpose of isolating the delinquent State internationally to restore the status quo ante.

B. The Discretionary Character of Acts of Recognition

States are not required to reveal their intentions or to give reasons for their actions. The absence of explicit public reaction, by third States and IOs, to a claim to statehood (or governmental authority), or a new territorial claim made by an existing State, presents commentators with a significant quandary – how should such silence be interpreted? There is the additional difficulty, in relation to the operation of the duty of non-recognition, of how to identify practice in support of a prohibition. No third State (or IO) is under a legal duty to recognise the creation of a new State or government, or to endorse a novel territorial claim made by an existing State. Third States and IOs may decide to perform acts of recognition for purely political reasons. Equally, these actors may choose to abjure a formal approach to recognition in favour of a policy by which recognition may be inferred from any bilateral dealings they may have with a new State/government or with an existing State in relation to territory over which it is claiming sovereignty. Consequently, in the absence of an explicit public declaration of recognition, it may be difficult for observers to work out the position adopted by a given third State or IO in relation to a novel situation, particularly in the short term, because any apparent inactivity may flow from either: the operation of the doctrine of implied recognition; the withholding of recognition on political grounds; or pursuant to a legal duty of non-recognition.

Third States might choose to take a critical attitude towards an established State's contentious territorial claim, culminating in the adoption of resolutions in various regional and/or IOs which express international concern about the targeted State's recalcitrant conduct. In particularly egregious cases,

27 However, see the powerful Dissenting Opinions of Judges Weeramantry and Skubiszewski addressing this issue (n 11) and (n 15) above.

28 See Talmon (n 4) 121.

third States may choose to support the adoption of targeted resolutions in the Security Council or General Assembly harnessing the language of international law concerning fundamental principles (e.g., sovereignty, use of force, territorial integrity, self-determination, etc). Nonetheless, such resolutions might avoid invoking a duty of non-recognition in the situation in issue. In such circumstances, attention will inevitably focus on any ongoing bilateral arrangements and dealings between individual States/IOs and the targeted State – especially those which relate to the territory that is the subject of a sovereignty claim – for the purpose of assessing whether they have impliedly recognised the controversial claim.

C. Formalism and Implied Recognition

The process of divining international legal obligations from instances of flagrant wrongdoing which have produced an illegal situation is fraught with difficulty as far as third States and IOs are concerned, especially when the Security Council is unwilling or unable to act. This problem is exacerbated by the fact that the act of recognition of an unlawful situation created in violation of *jus cogens* is not restricted to occasions where a third State or IO expressly recognises a claim made by a State or entity. Instead, as previously noted, dealings between the targeted State/entity and the third State or IO in question may be capable of implying recognition of the lawfulness of the situation. But if, as has long been supposed, recognition is both an intentional and discretionary act,[29] then, for doctrinal purposes, it is vital to be able to distinguish conduct which amounts to recognition from bilateral intercourse which falls short of that threshold. Such an approach assumes that a certain level or kind of bilateral dealing can be equated with an intention to recognise on the part of third States and IOs; however, the evidence in favour of the existence of such a categorical proposition is far from clear.

It has been argued that the duty of non-recognition may be satisfied by the making of a formal statement by a third State (or IO), stipulating that it does not recognise the lawfulness of the wrongdoing State's actions in a particular situation.[30] Consequently, it has been suggested that evidence from which recognition on the part of a third State may be inferred cannot be adduced

29 See James Crawford, *Brownlie's Principles of Public International Law* (9th ed, OUP 2019) 139; Malcolm Shaw, *International Law* (9th ed, CUP 2021) 385 and 395; Arthur Watts and Robert Jennings (eds) *Oppenheim's International Law*, Vol. 1 (9th ed, OUP 1992) 169; and Thomas Grant, 'How to Recognise a State (and Not)' in Christine Chinkin and Freya Baetens (eds), *Sovereignty, Statehood and State Responsibility: Essays in Honour of James Crawford* (CUP 2013) 192–208, 193 and 198.

30 The UK has expressed the view that the duty of non-recognition may amount to a 'barren' obligation: comments and observations submitted by the UK on Article 18 of the Draft Declaration on Rights and Duties of States, A/CN.4/2 (15 Dec 1948), 111, cited by Martin Dawidowicz, 'The

for such a purpose if the third State (or IO) in question has formally declared that it does not recognise the lawfulness of the wrongdoer's conduct in that setting. This approach is premised on the reasoning that recognition may only be implied when a third State or IO intends to recognise a concrete situation as being lawful without expressly so doing.[31] It has been observed that such a formalistic approach is a mistaken one because it confuses situations where a decision is made to withhold recognition on political grounds with cases where a legal duty of non-recognition has arisen.[32] However, the extent to which such a clear distinction can be drawn in practice is questionable given: (a) the difficulty in making sense of the intentions of States and IOs by reference to their conduct (unless those intentions have been declared by their representatives); and (b) the enduring uncertainty about whether a duty of non-recognition emerges in a concrete setting by the prior decision of the Security Council (or ICJ) or it falls to be determined by individual States/IOs through the ordinary process of customary international law.

The formalist approach to the duty of non-recognition is apparent from the 1970 Declaration on Friendly Relations, which provides inter alia that: 'No territorial acquisition resulting from the threat or use of force shall be recognized as legal'.[33] The 'as legal' formulation was designed to separate the illegality of a concrete instance of territorial annexation from its consequences.[34] This approach requires third States and IOs to withhold the imprimatur of legality from the wrongdoer's conduct while allowing them to accept the reality of the new territorial situation. If the wrongdoer manages to achieve and maintain effective control of the unlawfully annexed territory, third parties will be able to deal with that State or entity notwithstanding the fact that they have not accepted the lawfulness of the way in which it acquired the 'authority' to act in respect of the territory in question.[35] This approach is helped by the drawing of a distinction between non-recognition and 'cognition' in such situations.[36]

Talmon has pointed out that the ICJ was not prepared to embrace the formalist position in its *Namibia* Advisory Opinion, which was handed down the year after the Declaration on Friendly Relations was adopted.[37] He therefore casts doubt on the value of the 'as legal' formulation as a means of severely

Obligation of Non-Recognition of an Unlawful Situation', in James Crawford, Alain Pellet, and Simon Olleson (eds), *The Law of International Responsibility* (OUP 2010) 677, 679.

31 Grant (n 29) 198–199.

32 See James Crawford, *The Creation of States in International Law* (2nd ed, OUP 2006) 157–158.

33 See Talmon (n 4) 108–111.

34 Crawford acknowledges that the legality of an unlawful act may be denied but an actor may be bound to accept all or some of the consequences flowing from it: (n 32) 158.

35 See Pert (n 12) 17–18; Stefan Talmon, 'The Constitutive Versus the Declaratory Theory of Recognition: *Tertium Non Datur*?' (2004) 75 *BYIL* 101, 144–148.

36 Brownlie (n 20) 204–205; and Watts and Jennings (n 29) 154–157.

37 Talmon (n 4) 112.

curtailing the doctrine of non-recognition in practice. It is recalled that the ICJ provided some guidance regarding the kind of conduct which may be sufficient to imply recognition in that case.[38] It observed that States were under an obligation to abstain from performing existing bilateral treaties concluded with South Africa concerning Namibia.[39] The Court added that States were also under a duty to refrain from entering into economic arrangements, and other relations, with South Africa which may have the effect of entrenching its authority in respect of this Territory (including the maintenance of diplomatic and consular missions there).[40] The ICJ's rulings in this case were made in response to an illegal situation created by South Africa's flagrant violation of international law, which had already prompted the General Assembly to withdraw its authority to act as the Territory's mandatory power and the Security Council to adopt a number of resolutions concerning the illegal situation which emerged in Namibia, including resolution 276 (1970), which formed the subject matter of the request for the Advisory Opinion. The ICJ ruled that South Africa's behaviour triggered *erga omnes* obligations for third States barring them from endorsing the legality of the exercise of its governmental authority in respect of Namibia.[41] Nonetheless, it conceded that third States may not be in breach of the duty of non-recognition if they have accepted certain acts of public administration conducted by the unrecognised regime, which are beneficial to the Territory's inhabitants.[42]

The approach to the duty of non-recognition adopted in the *Namibia* Opinion did not result in the 'as legal/as lawful' formulation being jettisoned. For instance, Article 5(3) of the 1974 Definition of Aggression provides that: 'No territorial acquisition or special advantage resulting from aggression is or shall be recognized as lawful'.[43] Moreover, the 'as lawful' formulation also found its way into Article 41(2) of the ARSIWA.[44] Against this background, it is unclear whether it is still possible for a third State or IO to disavow formally the lawfulness of the target State's behaviour in a particular territorial

38 See Crawford (n 32) 183.

39 *Namibia* Advisory Opinion, para 122.

40 ibid., 123–124.

41 In the Court's own words: 'the termination of the Mandate and the declaration of the illegality of South Africa's presence in Namibia are opposable to all States in the sense of barring *erga omnes* the legality of a situation which is maintained in violation of international law', para 126.

42 The 'Namibia exception' is set out in para 125. Crawford suggested that it applies to acts untainted by the illegal character of the administration which has performed them: (n 32) 164. The Court also observed that States were still under an obligation to observe the terms of multilateral treaties of a humanitarian character notwithstanding the illegal nature of the regime in question: (para 122).

43 UNGA Res 3314 (XXIX) (1974).

44 This formalist strategy was advocated by Australia during the oral proceedings in the *East Timor* Case even though its veracity was not tested by the ICJ on that occasion. See oral proceedings in the *East Timor* Case, CR.95/14 (16 February 1995) 36, para 5. See Pert (n 12) 18 and Milano (n 10) 50.

context while having substantial and extensive bilateral dealings with that State relating to the situation in issue. However, if recognition is essentially a matter of intention, then the scope for such an approach cannot be easily dismissed. Arguably, this has been demonstrated through the litigation instituted in response to successive trade and fishing agreements concluded between the EU and Morocco.

(i) EU/Morocco Trade and Fishing Agreements and Implied Recognition

Notwithstanding Morocco's continuing presence and actions in Western Sahara, certain third parties have concluded and implemented treaties with Morocco concerning the exploitation of natural resources belonging to the people of Western Sahara in violation of international law. For instance, the European Union and Morocco have concluded a series of trade and fishing agreements, which have been systematically applied to Western Sahara (and its adjacent waters).[45] Such bilateral arrangements have prompted the question of whether such conduct constitutes implied recognition of Morocco's sovereign claim to Western Sahara. Many commentators have argued that the EU's sustained and extensive dealings with Morocco regarding natural resources originating in Western Sahara or in the Territory's adjacent waters are tantamount to implied recognition.[46] However, the EU Council and Commission have steadfastly maintained that they have not recognised Morocco's sovereignty claim to Western Sahara and the EU courts have not ruled otherwise in those cases which have come before them.[47]

The *Western Sahara Campaign* Case concerned a successful challenge to the 2006 EU/Morocco Fishing Partnership Agreement (FPA), and its 2013 Protocol which enabled the EU's fleet to engage in extensive fishing activities in the waters adjacent to Western Sahara and Morocco.[48] The decision of the Court of Justice of the European Union (CJEU) in this case was substantially informed by its earlier judgment in *Council v Polisario*, a tariff privileges challenge to the application of successive EU/Morocco trade agreements to

45 There have also been similar fishing agreements concluded between Morocco and Russia regarding fishing activities in the waters adjacent to Western Sahara.

46 See, e.g., Martin Dawidowicz, 'Trading Fish or Human Rights in Western Sahara' in D. French (ed), *Statehood and Self-Determination* (CUP 2013); Eva Kassoti, 'Between Völkerrechtsfreundlichkeit and Realpolitik: The EU and Trade Agreements covering Occupied Territories' (2016) 26 *ItYIL* 139; and Eva Kassoti, 'The EU's duty of non-recognition and the territorial scope of trade agreements covering unlawfully acquired territories' (2019) 3(1): 5 *Europe and the World: A Law Review* 1–18.

47 See Stephen Allen, 'Exploiting Non-Self-Governing Territory Status: Western Sahara and the New EU/Morocco Sustainable Fisheries Partnership Agreement' (2020) 9(1) *CILJ* 24–50.

48 Case C-266/16 *R (Western Sahara Campaign UK) v HMRC & Secretary of State for the Environment* [2018] EU:C:2018:18.

Western Sahara.[49] In both these cases, the CJEU chose to harness the principle of self-determination and Western Sahara's separate status as a NSGT to address the de facto application of the EU/Morocco agreements to Western Sahara along with the customary international law principle of *pacta tertiis nec nocent nec prosunt*, which holds that a treaty cannot create rights and/or duties for a third party without its consent.[50] As the people of Western Sahara had not consented to the application of EU/Morocco treaties to Western Sahara and its adjacent waters through their legitimate representative – the Polisario – the Court ruled that the treaties were inapplicable to Western Sahara.

It is notable that the CJEU chose not to invoke the doctrine of recognition in its judgments, preferring instead to remain within the parameters of the principles of self-determination and consent. However, in these cases, Advocate-General Wathelet was prepared to consider the question of whether the EU has impliedly recognised Morocco's claim to Western Sahara by concluding treaties which were being applied to this Territory and/or its waters. In his 2016 Opinion in *Council v Polisario*, he wrote that it was impossible to reconcile the application of the EU/Morocco trade agreements to Western Sahara without arriving at the conclusion that the EU had impliedly recognised Morocco's sovereignty claim to that Territory.[51] Further, in his 2018 Opinion in the *Western Sahara Campaign* Case, Advocate-General Wathelet was unable to accept the argument that the EU/Morocco fisheries agreements could fall within the scope of the Namibia 'exception' because, in his view, it did not extend to international agreements of this kind.[52]

The EU Commission and Council wanted to find a way of maintaining the EU fishing fleet's access to the abundant fishing area adjacent to Western Sahara. Accordingly, the EU/Morocco Sustainable Fishing Partnership Agreement (SFPA) was negotiated in response to the CJEU's judgment in the *Western Sahara Campaign* Case and it was adopted by the EU Council in March 2019.[53] In an Exchange of Letters accompanying the SFPA,[54] the EU and Morocco set out their respective 'without prejudice' positions

49 Case C-104/16P *Council v Front Polisario* [2016] EU:C:2016:973.

50 The principle is now codified in Article 34 of the Vienna Convention on the Law of Treaties (1969) 1155 UNTS 331.

51 Advocate-General Wathelet's Opinion, Case 104/16P, paras 84–86.

52 Advocate-General Wathelet's Opinion, Case C-266/16, paras 288–292.

53 Council Decision (EU) 2019/441 of 4 March 2019 on the conclusion of the Sustainable Fisheries Partnership Agreement between the European Union and the Kingdom of Morocco, the Implementation Protocol thereto and the Exchange of Letters accompanying the Agreement [2019] OJ L77/4.

54 Exchange of Letters between the European Union and the Kingdom of Morocco accompanying the Sustainable Fisheries Partnership Agreement between the European Union and the Kingdom of Morocco [2019] OJ L 77/53. The Exchange of Letters forms an integral part of the SFPA, according to Articles 1(c) and 16 SFPA.

concerning the status of Western Sahara.[55] According to the EU, any references in the treaty to Moroccan laws and regulations did not affect Western Sahara's NSGT status; 'its' right to self-determination;[56] or the EU's view that the Territory's waters constitute part of the material fishing zone. Morocco, in contrast, maintained that it exercises full sovereignty over 'the Sahara region'.[57] Despite these radically diverging views regarding the legal status of the material fishing zone, the EU Council has denied that there is anything in the SFPA which would imply that the EU recognises Morocco's sovereignty claim to Western Sahara and its adjacent waters (or to exercise any sovereign rights therein).[58] During the process of adopting the SFPA, it reiterated the EU's formal position on the Western Sahara Question:

> The Union does not prejudice the outcome of the political process on the final status of Western Sahara taking place under the auspices of the United Nations, and it has constantly reaffirmed its commitment to the settlement of the dispute in Western Sahara, which is currently listed by the United Nations as a non-self-governing territory and administered principally by the Kingdom of Morocco. It fully supports the efforts made by the United Nations Secretary-General and his personal envoy to assist the parties in achieving a just, lasting and mutually acceptable political solution which will allow the self-determination of the people of Western Sahara as part of arrangements consistent with the purposes and principles set out in the Charter of the United Nations and enshrined in United Nations Security Council resolutions.[59]

The content and application of successive EU/Morocco fishing agreements to the waters adjacent to Western Sahara reveals the persistent lack of clarity regarding the nature and extent of bilateral dealings from which recognition may be implied as far as third States and IOs are concerned, contrary to the approach adopted by the ICJ in its *Namibia* Advisory Opinion. In addition, given those treaties, the EU Council's formal position on the Western Sahara Question demonstrates that recognition remains a matter of intention and its essential character leaves plenty of room for opportunistic third States and IOs to pursue instrumental strategies despite the duty of non-recognition's perceived communitarian nature.[60]

55 ibid.

56 This entitlement inheres in the people of the NSGT, rather than belonging to the Territory itself.

57 See the General Court's two separate Judgments (29 September 2021) in *Front Polisario v Council*, Cases T-344/19 and T-356/19 (SFPA challenge); and *Front Polisario v Council*, Case 279/19 (trade preferences challenge). The Council is currently appealing these cases to the CJEU.

58 EU Council Decision 2019/441, para 12.

59 EU Council Decision 2019/441, para 4.

60 See Milano (n 10) 47–48 and see Chapter V(A) below.

D. The Consequences of the Duty of Non-Recognition

Writing in the late 1940s, Lauterpacht saw non-recognition as a modest symbolic device that constituted the minimum level of resistance available against wrongdoing in international law.[61] He thought the fact that a duty of non-recognition had emerged would not necessarily prevent the maintenance of ordinary relations between the wrongdoer and third States, including the conclusion and observance of bilateral treaty relations inter se, notwithstanding the existence of an illegal situation which contravened the *ex injuria jus non oritur* principle.[62] According to Lauterpacht, the withholding of recognition of the lawfulness of such situations was merely a way of bringing pressure to bear on the wrongdoing State to ensure the cessation of its transgressive behaviour while maintaining the formal integrity of international law for the time being.[63] For him, the duty of non-recognition sought to prevent an unlawful factual situation from giving rise to law-creating consequences rather than seeking to deny political reality in a particular setting.[64]

However, from the 1960s onwards, international law began to follow a more communitarian approach to certain global problems as demonstrated, in the colonial context, by the Security Council's strong reaction to the unilateral declaration of independence by a minority racist regime in Southern Rhodesia and the measures taken by the Security Council, General Assembly, and the ICJ in response to South Africa's delinquent behaviour in Namibia.[65] In 1992, Jennings and Watts observed that, in the absence of contrary evidence, the conclusion of a bilateral treaty would be tantamount to recognition of the target State.[66] This reasoning would extend to situations where the agreement related to territory controversially claimed by an established State.[67] However, more recently, Shaw has taken a more tentative approach, observing that one would need to evaluate all the circumstances carefully before deciding whether a given bilateral treaty constituted decisive evidence of an intention to recognise in any given case.[68] This standpoint may be informed by the growing complexity and flexibility of treaty relations in contemporary international law,[69] as illustrated by the fishing agreements concluded between the EU and Morocco, discussed in Section C(i) above.

61 Lauterpacht (n 4) 431.

62 ibid., 432–433.

63 ibid., 427 and 430.

64 ibid., 430.

65 Discussed in Chapter III(A) above.

66 Watts and Jennings (n 29) 171, 174.

67 Ibid. 175 and 200.

68 See Shaw (n 29) 394; and Toby Fenwick, 'The Seychelles-Somaliland Prisoner Transfer Agreement: A Case of Implicit Recognition?' (2019) 27:3 *AfrJIntl&CompL* 400–425.

69 See Daniel Costelloe, *Legal Consequences of Peremptory Norms in International Law* (CUP 2017) chapter 2.

The communitarian commitment is deeply embedded in the concepts of *jus cogens* and *erga omnes*.[70] *Erga omnes* obligations flow from the standpoint that every State has a legal interest in ensuring that communitarian norms are upheld.[71] As previously mentioned, in its *Namibia* Advisory Opinion, the ICJ concluded that third States were barred from facilitating the *erga omnes* legality of South Africa's presence and actions in Namibia. Later, in its *Wall* Advisory Opinion, the ICJ acknowledged that the concept of *erga omnes* could extend to *rights* as well as obligations in certain situations.[72] In that case, the ICJ accepted that the Palestinian people possess an *erga omnes* right to self-determination, which third States are bound to respect. As a result, the beneficiaries of the right to self-determination (here, the Palestinian people) have a direct claim against the State which is under the principal obligation to facilitate its exercise (i.e., Israel). However, the obligation of third States is to respect the right to self-determination of the people concerned.[73] Such differentiation raises the question of how the obligation *erga omnes* to respect the right in issue can be satisfied. Pert thinks it is a mistake to compare a situation where the principal wrongdoer violates a peremptory norm with a scenario in which a third State breaches the obligation of non-recognition by dealing with the wrongdoer in some way.[74] She rightly points out that the principal wrongdoer would clearly bear international responsibility, pursuant to Articles 40 and 41 of the ARSIWA, since it has violated *jus cogens*. However, in such a scenario, Pert suggests the third State's conduct amounts to a breach of customary international law and so the communitarian norms set out in Chapter 3 of the ARSIWA are not activated. The duty of non-recognition is a norm of customary international law but, as Talmon argues, in situations where it is activated, third States and IOs are required to abstain positively from dealing with the principal wrongdoer regarding the illegal situation in question, otherwise they are violating the obligation *erga omnes* to respect the right of self-determination of the people concerned.[75] On this reading, self-determination's *erga omnes* character has strengthened the scope for enforcing the customary obligation of non-recognition in situations where it is engaged.

(i) Persistent Illegal Situations and Territorial Claims

Lauterpacht observed long ago that a tension exists between the principles of *ex injuria jus non oritur* and *ex factis jus oritur* (the facts create the law)

70 See Crawford (n 3) 362–390.

71 See Article 48 ARSIWA and the *Barcelona Traction* Case (Second Phase) [1970] ICJ Reps 3, 32, para 33.

72 See *Wall* Advisory Opinion (2004), paras 155–156;

73 Yoshifumi Tanaka, 'The Legal Consequences of Obligations *Erga Omnes* in International Law' (2021) 68 *Netherlands International Law Review* (2021) 1, 7.

74 Pert (n 12) 19–21.

75 Talmon (n 4) 112.

in cases where the unlawful situation has endured for a considerable period. In such circumstances, Lauterpacht anticipated that the law would have to give way to changes occurring over time since it could not remain impervious to the facts.[76] This approach was subsequently endorsed by Jennings in the context of territorial acquisition.[77] Wilde recounts Jennings' observation that a dubious claim to territory, which has been acquired through the unlawful use of force, might be cured 'through recognitions or other forms of the position expressive of the will of the international community'.[78] Wilde suggests that the availability of such a remedy is attributable to the rules of orthodox positive international law which are grounded in the consent of States.[79] Nevertheless, he acknowledges that Jennings was writing before the advent of *jus cogens* norms and obligations *erga omnes*. Notwithstanding these latter-day communitarian developments, Wilde worries that State practice contrary to the prohibitions on the use of force and the denial of the right to self-determination could still lead to the erosion of fundamental international norms.[80]

Tanaka suggests the significance of the obligation of non-recognition is minimal when the factual ambitions of the wrongdoer have already been achieved since the wrongdoer cannot acquire good title to the territory in question anyway by virtue of the principle of *ex injuria jus non oritur*.[81] Orakhelashvili takes a more conceptual approach. He argues that peremptory norms can only be modified by a subsequent norm of the same character and so the ordinary law-generating processes could not displace a *jus cogens* norm.[82] The prohibition on the use of force for the purpose of annexing territory and the right of self-determination have undoubtedly acquired *jus cogens* status. Accordingly, on this reasoning, it is extremely difficult to argue that persistent control of occupied territory can do anything to cure the illegality of the situation in question. Moreover, if third States are indeed required to refrain from recognising the lawfulness of such a situation, then it is not possible to claim that they have acquiesced in response to the wrongdoer's behaviour. Nevertheless, international relations must continue in some form with the recalcitrant State, especially where that State exerts considerable regional or global influence. In such circumstances, a search for a negotiated political solution will inevitably be required and it is at this point that international

76 Lauterpacht (n 4) 426–427.
77 Robert Y. Jennings, *The Acquisition of Territory in International Law* (Manchester University Press; Oceana Publications, 1962) 62–64.
78 Ralph Wilde quoted from the 2017 reprint of Jennings' book, at 84 (67 in the original), in 'Using the Master's Tools to Dismantle the Master's House: International Law and Palestinian Liberation' (2019–2020) 22 *PalYIL* 3–74, 68.
79 ibid. 70.
80 Wilde (n 78) 67–70.
81 Tanaka (n 73) 14–15.
82 See Orakhelashvili (n 2) 127.

law's specific contribution becomes harder to gauge, as illustrated by the Western Sahara Question.[83]

(ii) The African Court's Judgment in the Bernard Mornah Case

The consequences of the people of Western Sahara's right to self-determination for African Union (AU) members were considered by the African Court on Human and Peoples' Rights in the *Bernard Mornah* Case.[84] It considered whether the Respondent States had breached any obligations which they owed to the Sahrawi people, pursuant to the right to self-determination, by having voted in favour of Morocco's admission to the AU in 2017.[85] To this end, it examined the alleged denial of the Sahrawi people's entitlement to self-determination as a result of Morocco's protracted occupation of Western Sahara/ the Sahrawi Arab Democratic Republic (SADR) by recourse to the provisions of the African Charter and general international law, with a view to establishing whether such conduct could give rise to international responsibility on the part of the Respondent States.[86]

At the outset, the African Court appreciated that the right to self-determination generates differentiated obligations for the principal wrongdoer and third States/IOs. Specifically, it drew a distinction between the conduct of the Respondent States in the context of the proceedings and that of Morocco, 'which is alleged to have directly violated the rights of the Sahrawi people through occupation'.[87] It went on to explain the significance of the right to self-determination for African peoples by recourse to Article 20 of the African Charter on Human and Peoples' Rights, which provides that:

(1) All peoples shall have the right to existence. They shall have the unquestionable and inalienable right to self-determination. They shall freely determine their political status and shall pursue their economic and social development according to the policy they have freely chosen.
(2) Colonized and oppressed peoples shall have the right to free themselves from the bonds of domination by resorting to any means recognized by the international community.

83 See Theodore Christakis and Aristoteles Constantinides, 'Territorial Disputes in the Context of Secessionist Conflicts', in Marcelo Kohen and Mamadou Hébié, *Research Handbook on Territorial Disputes in International Law* (Elgar 2018) 343–395, 358.

84 Judgment of 22 September 2022, on Application 028/2018.

85 The Respondent States were Benin, Burkina Faso, Ivory Coast, Ghana, Mali, Malawi, Tanzania, and Tunisia. These were the States that had made declarations under Article 34 of the Protocol to the African Charter, accepting the Court's jurisdiction in cases brought by individuals.

86 Judgment paras 283–287.

87 ibid., para 288.

(3) All peoples shall have the right to assistance of the State Parties to the present Charter in their liberation struggle against foreign domination, be it political, economic or cultural.[88]

The Court observed that, in the light of this provision, self-determination has gained special resonance in the African context.[89] The Court reaffirmed self-determination's status as a peremptory norm of general international law, which has given rise to an *erga omnes* obligation as far as all States are concerned.[90] Consequently, it acknowledged that third States are under a duty not to recognise an illegal situation arising from the breach of a peremptory norm and are required to refrain from aiding or assisting the principal wrongdoer in the maintenance of such a situation.[91]

The Court then turned to contemplate the contention that the people of the SADR/Western Sahara have been deprived of their ability to exercise their right to self-determination due to Morocco's occupation of the Territory.[92] In this context, it observed that: 'both the UN and the AU recognise the situation of SADR as one of occupation and consider its territory as one of those territories whose decolonisation process is not yet fully complete'.[93] The Court noted that Morocco's assertion of sovereignty over Western Sahara, 'has never been accepted by the international community'.[94] It endorsed the ICJ's conclusion, in its *Western Sahara* Advisory Opinion, that Morocco's historical claim to Western Sahara did not affect the application of the principle of self-determination as far as the Territory's decolonisation was concerned.[95] The African Court, therefore, decided to take judicial notice of the validity of the SADR's sovereignty claim.[96] Accordingly, it found Morocco's occupation of the SADR's territory to be incompatible with the right to self-determination, as enumerated in Article 20 of the African Charter.[97]

The fact that the African Court decided to characterise Morocco's presence in Western Sahara as an 'occupation' which is incompatible with the Sahrawi people's right to self-determination is remarkable. It was mindful to use the language of incompatibility rather than violation, but its signalling on

88 ibid., paras 288, 293, 295, 299, 303.

89 ibid., paras 293–295. It harnessed the constitutional documents of the OAU and AU as well as the principles of customary international law in this regard, paras 288–295.

90 ibid., paras 297–299.

91 ibid. It is also appreciated that the obligation to respect the right to self-determination manifests an extra-territorial aspect because Article 20(3) of the African Charter is unconstrained by geographical considerations.

92 ibid., para 300.

93 ibid., para 301.

94 ibid., para 302.

95 ibid.

96 ibid.

97 Ibid., para 303.

this issue could not have been clearer. It is true that the UN General Assembly has twice referred to Morocco's presence in Western Sahara as an occupation.[98] However, it has been more than 40 years since the Assembly last used this term in relation to the Western Sahara Question and it has adopted a much more conciliatory approach in recent years.[99] Further, as previously noted, the Security Council has never described Morocco's presence in the Territory as amounting to an occupation. In this context, it is recalled that when UN Secretary-General Ban Ki Moon used the term 'occupation' in reference to the situation prevailing in Western Sahara during a speech made on a regional tour in 2016, the Council failed to support him, and the Moroccan government's strong reaction led to the virtual dismantling of the civilian component of the UN Mission for the Referendum in Western Sahara (MINURSO) for a time thereafter.[100]

The Court noted that parties to the African Charter were not only subject to an international legal obligation to refrain from taking steps that were incompatible with the enjoyment of the right to self-determination, but they were required to take positive measures to facilitate the realisation of this right.[101] It indicated that States parties were also under a duty, individually and collectively, to assist the Sahrawi people in their struggle for freedom as well as to refrain from recognising Morocco's occupation of the SADR's territory/Western Sahara.[102] Against this background, the African Court explained that its specific task was to determine: 'whether the Respondent States [...] have shirked their responsibility in the Charter by either failing to give assistance to the people of SADR or by recognising the illegal occupation by Morocco of the SADR's territory contrary to the people's right to self-determination [...]'.[103] Notwithstanding the Court's detailed exposition of Article 20 of the African Charter, it conceded that it was for the States parties themselves to decide which measures to adopt for this purpose.[104] In this regard, the Court observed that all the Respondent States had supported the ongoing diplomatic efforts of both the UN and the AU to resolve this dispute. As a result, it concluded that the Respondents had not failed to discharge their obligation to assist the Sahrawi people, as required by the Charter.[105] The Court seemed to have been aware of the weakness of this conclusion since it reflected that 'one may still question the adequacy of [the Respondents'] measures' in

98 See UNGA Res 34/37 (21 November 1979) and UNGA Res 35/19 (11 November 1980).

99 See Chapter IV(B)(ii) below.

100 See UN Security Council 'What's in Blue' (17 March 2016); UNSC Monthly Forecast Report (April 2016); and the Secretary-General's Report on Western Sahara S/2016/355 (19 April 2016) paras 2–4.

101 Judgment para 305.

102 ibid., para 317.

103 ibid., para 308.

104 ibid., para 314.

105 ibid., para 315.

this respect.[106] Ultimately, the Court held that, in accordance with the procedures set out in Article 29(2) of the AU's Constitutive Act, the admission of a State to membership is to be decided by a simple majority of the member States.[107] Thus, as the individual decisions of the Respondent States regarding Morocco's admission would not necessarily determine the matter, it ruled that any such decisions could not constitute a breach of obligations generated by the African Charter or arising from general international law.[108] Essentially, the Court ruled that decisions about membership were taken by the AU's Assembly, which possesses its own separate legal personality that is distinct from individual member States.[109]

In the end, the Court decided not to pronounce on any of the alleged human rights violations flowing from Morocco's occupation of Western Sahara as Morocco was not a party to the proceedings.[110] This position sits rather uncomfortably with the Court's willingness to take judicial notice of Morocco's occupation of a substantial part of SADR/Western Saharan territory earlier in its judgment.[111] The Court decided that there was no causal connection between the human rights violations alleged by the Applicant and the actions of the Respondents.[112] In its view, they had not violated the Sahrawi people's right to self-determination, and the act of voting in favour of Morocco's admission by itself did not amount to recognition of Morocco's occupation of SADR territory.[113] The Court felt the need to add that AU member States:

> had to find a permanent solution to the occupation and to ensure the enjoyment of the inalienable right to self-determination of the Sahrawi people and not to do anything that would give recognition to such occupation as lawful or impede their enjoyment of this right.[114]

This hollow statement is arguably consistent with the infamous charge that the duty of non-recognition is an obligation without substance.[115] In any event, the Court's analysis of this duty does not inspire confidence as far as the realisation of the Sahrawi people's right to self-determination is concerned.

106 ibid.
107 ibid., paras 317–318.
108 ibid., para 318.
109 ibid., para 319.
110 ibid., para 321. Earlier in its judgment, the Court was careful to state that: 'Morocco's conduct is not subject to the Court's determination as Morocco is not a party in this case', para 288.
111 See the discussion above accompanying ns 96 and 97, above.
112 Judgment para 321.
113 ibid., paras 319, 320 and 322.
114 ibid., para 323.
115 See the Separate Opinion of Judge Kooijmans in the *Wall* Advisory Opinion, para 44.

4 Recent Developments in UN Practice Concerning Western Sahara

There have been discernible shifts in the way in which the UN's principal organs, and their member States, have approached the settlement of this dispute in recent years, a development which appears to have been accelerated by the resumption of the armed conflict between Morocco and the Polisario since November 2020. In particular, there has been growing support within the UN for Morocco's autonomy plan, which is founded on the acceptance that Morocco already exercises sovereignty over Western Sahara. Therefore, support for Morocco's autonomy plan amounts to an indirect endorsement of its sovereignty claim by sympathetic third States and International Organisations (IOs), notwithstanding the need for a negotiated settlement. Certain States have gone further by endorsing Morocco's sovereignty claim in explicit terms within UN fora (and elsewhere) and a few States have invoked the doctrine of recognition while providing such direct support. This chapter examines the positions advanced by third States when participating in meetings of the Security Council and in the General Assembly's committees concerning the Western Sahara Question as well as the resolutions of these UN organs with a view to assessing the extent to which, by supporting Morocco's autonomy plan, third States are now prepared to accept its claim to Western Sahara. This prompts a consideration of whether the endorsement of Morocco's sovereignty claim by certain States in UN proceedings amounts to recognition despite the fundamental norms engaged by the Western Sahara dispute.

The issue of Western Sahara has arisen as a source of controversy in many corners of the UN, not only within the Organisation's main organs. For instance, in early 2023 the Human Rights Council issued its report following the Universal Periodic Review of Morocco, which contained several conclusions and recommendations relating to human rights in Western Sahara, including the right to self-determination.[1] In response, Morocco resisted the notion that the right of self-determination applied in its 'southern provinces', and when seeking to underscore the normality of the situation in the territory, took the opportunity to note the presence of 'more than 30 diplomatic and

1 A/HRC/52/7, 22–23.

DOI: 10.4324/9781032658827-4

consular missions' there.[2] Morocco also rejected a recommendation that it should cooperate with the Secretary-General's Personal Envoy, on the basis that it fell outside the mandate of the Human Rights Council.[3]

A comprehensive survey of UN practice would need to factor in the work of many other organs and agencies across the Organisation and would quickly exceed the limits of this short book. The focus of this chapter will therefore be on the Security Council and General Assembly, where the most significant recent multilateral developments regarding Western Sahara have unfolded.

A. The Security Council's Approach to the Western Sahara Question Since 2018

The Security Council's engagement with the Western Sahara Question up until 2018 is discussed in Chapter 2(A)(ii). At this point, the USA decided to embark on a new policy approach to the Western Sahara Question. It sought to use its influence as the penholder of the 'Group of Friends on Western Sahara' to tie the renewal of the mandate of the UN Mission for the Referendum in Western Sahara (MINURSO) to the achievement of progress towards the settlement of the conflict.[4] To this end, certain substantive changes were introduced to the established formula used in successive resolutions on Western Sahara. Specifically, Security Council Resolution 2414 (27 April 2018), 'emphasize[d] the need to make progress towards a realistic, practical and enduring political solution to the question of Western Sahara based on compromise [...]'.[5] The resolution retained the call for the parties to resume good faith negotiations without preconditions to achieve a just, lasting, and mutually acceptable political solution providing for the self-determination of the people of Western Sahara, in a manner consistent with the UN Charter's principles and purposes.[6] It also reiterated the Council's long-standing endorsement of the Secretary-General's 2008 recommendation that negotiations should be conducted in the spirit of realism and compromise.[7] Nonetheless, the new approach signalled a radical shift of focus away from considerations of process towards the substantive outcomes of any negotiation solution.[8] The new approach provoked much consternation within the Council, prompting

2 ibid., 6–7.

3 A/HRC/52/7/Add.1/Morocco/Annex/E, 'The position of the Kingdom of Morocco on the recommendations issued during the consideration of the national report of the fourth cycle of the Universal Periodic Review' (February 2023, translated from the Arabic), para 20.

4 S/PV.8246th meeting (27 April 2018), p. 2.

5 SCR 2414, para 2. The resolution also stipulated that MINURSO's mandate would be extended for six months rather than the established practice of annual renewal.

6 SCR 2414 para 3.

7 SCR 2414, para 11.

8 South Africa's subsequent analysis of this change is discussed below.

China, Ethiopia, and Russia to abstain during the vote on Resolution 2414. They complained about the absence of consensus concerning the final text and its lack of balance.[9] Russia expressed deep concern about the introduction of the concepts of 'realism' and 'practicality'. It reasoned that this new language had the effect of undermining the Council's established approach and its impartiality as far as the Western Sahara Question was concerned.[10]

Resolutions 2440 (31 October 2018), 2468 (30 April 2019), and 2548 (30 October 2020), largely followed the same pattern.[11] After the vote on Resolution 2548, the USA's representative expressed her country's support for Morocco's autonomy plan so that the 'people of Western Sahara [are able] to run their own affairs with peace and dignity'.[12] In abstaining, South Africa contended that Resolution 2548 did not reflect the humanitarian and political security crises currently affecting Western Sahara.[13] It also drew attention to the lack of neutrality on the issue of Western Sahara by pointing to the Council's acknowledgement of Morocco's 'serious and credible efforts' to move the peace process forward by means of its autonomy proposal ever since Resolution 1754 (2007).[14] South Africa restated its opposition to the insertion of the terms 'realism', 'realistic', and 'compromise' into resolutions on Western Sahara since 2018.[15] It reminded the Council that although such language found its origins in the Secretary-General's 2008 recommendation, it was originally intended to refer to the process of negotiations rather than to any substantive outcomes arising from them. South Africa claimed that such 'ambiguous' terms could be construed as a need to accept political reality rather than to recognise the requirements of international legality concerning the settlement of the conflict.[16]

Despite the November 2020 Guerguerat crisis and the resumption of hostilities between the parties,[17] Resolution 2602 (29 October 2021), the Council's next resolution on Western Sahara, bore a remarkable similarity

9 S/PV.8246th meeting (27 April 2018) pp. 3–4 (Russia), p. 6 (China), and p. 8 (Bolivia).

10 SC 8246th meeting (27 April 2018) p 4.

11 Since Resolution 2494 (30 October 2019) the Council has reverted to its traditional practice of renewing MINURSO's mandate for 12 months, largely due to Kohler's resignation: See Secretary-General's Report S/2019/787 (2 October 2019) paras 77 and 89.

12 The Council's business was affected by the COVID-19 pandemic when Resolution 2548 was being considered. Through a letter dated 29 October 2020, the President of the Security Council tabled the resolution on the Western Sahara Question. Statements made by way of explanation of the votes recorded were annexed to the President's letter confirming the outcome of the vote. The USA's comments were contained in Annex 25, 32.

13 Annex 23, 29.

14 ibid., 30.

15 ibid.

16 ibid., 30.

17 See Chapter II(A)(iii) above.

to its immediate predecessor.[18] In the resolution's preamble, the Council expressed its 'concern about the violation of existing agreements [while] reiterating the importance of full adherence to these commitments'. However, it chose to repeat the same formula it had used in Resolution 2548 rather than accepting the ceasefire's demise. After the vote, the USA reiterated its view that Morocco's autonomy plan remains a 'serious, credible and realistic' initiative which could 'promote a peaceful and prosperous future for the people of the region' without mentioning the principle of self-determination at all.[19] Mexico chose to couch its support for the UN process by stating that the objective of the negotiating process remains the delivery of self-determination for the people of Western Sahara in keeping with the requirements of international law.[20] The Russian representative bemoaned the penholder's refusal to make significant revisions to the draft resolution based on proposals made by Council members which meant that the final resolution 'does not reflect the objective picture of what has happened on the Western Sahara issue following the military escalation in November [2020]'.[21] He repeated his country's criticism of ambiguous textual references to 'the need to abide by the so-called "realistic" approaches or to make some compromises' adding that such a formulation undermines trust in the Council's work, and it makes the resumption of dialogue harder.[22]

In his 2022 Report on Western Sahara, the Secretary-General set out the key activities of his new Personal Envoy, Staffan de Mistura, during the period.[23] He recounted de Mistura's meetings with the four interested parties (Morocco, the Polisario, Algeria, and Mauritania), members of the Group of Friends and other stakeholders, while drawing attention to several worrying developments as far as the peace process is concerned. The Secretary-General noted Morocco's insistence that its autonomy proposal provides the exclusive basis for discussions between the four interested parties,[24] the Algerian government's resistance to the use of the continued roundtable format,[25] and the deterioration in relations between Morocco and Algeria.[26] Further,

18 Resolution 2602 (29 October 2021) adopted at the Council's 8890th meeting. Russia and Tunisia abstained on this occasion.

19 S/PV.8890, p. 2.

20 ibid., p. 3. The French representative noted that MINURSO's role was vital to ensuring regional stability and he called on the parties to respect the ceasefire while reaffirming his country's support for Morocco's autonomy plan (p. 3).

21 S/PV.8890, p. 3.

22 S/PV.8890, p. 3.

23 Secretary-General's Report on the situation in Western Sahara (S/2022/733, 3 October 2022) paras 20-31. De Mistura took up his post on 1 November 2021, and visited the Territory for the first time on 4 September 2023.

24 ibid., para 26.

25 ibid., para 25.

26 ibid., para 93.

the Secretary-General discussed the Spanish government's recent decision to endorse Morocco's autonomy proposal, quoting a letter, dated 14 March 2021, in which the Spanish Prime Minister indicated to the Moroccan King that the proposal provides 'the most serious, credible, and realistic basis for resolving the dispute'.[27] This event signalled a move away from Spain's establish position of 'active neutrality' as far as the Western Sahara Question is concerned.[28] The Secretary-General added that his Envoy had been subsequently assured, by the Spanish Foreign Minister, that his country's support for the UN-facilitated process was unaffected by this policy change.[29]

On 22 October 2022, the Security Council adopted Resolution 2654 by which it renewed MINURSO's mandate for another twelve months.[30] The resolution's preamble noted the breakdown of the ceasefire 'with deep concern'. It focused on the violation of the military agreements both sides had concluded with the UN and called for full compliance with those commitments.[31] It also recognised the vital 'role played by MINURSO on the ground and the need for it to conduct the safe and regular resupply of its team sites, to conduct patrols throughout its area of responsibility, and to fully implement its mandate [...]'. The Council stressed 'the need to achieve a realistic, practicable, enduring and mutually acceptable political solution [...]' in keeping with its new approach,[32] while maintaining its established support for

> the parties to resume negotiations [...] without preconditions and in good faith [...] with a view to achieving a just, lasting, and mutually acceptable political solution, which will provide for the self-determination of the people of Western Sahara in the context of arrangements consistent with the principles and purposes of the [UN] Charter.[33]

Moreover, it called on the parties to ensure that the Mission's personnel have the freedom of movement, access, and security needed for it to fulfil its mandate while enabling 'the safe and regular resupply of MINURSO team sites', thereby maintaining 'the sustainability of the Mission's presence' in the Territory.[34]

27 ibid., para 13.
28 Security Council Report Monthly Forecast (October 2022), p. 16. Spain's recent change of position is discussed in more detail in Chapter V below.
29 This assurance was given during a meeting held on 21 March 2022, SG's Report (n 23) para 13.
30 S/PV.9168 (27 October 2022). It was adopted by 13 votes with two abstentions (Kenya and Russia).
31 Resolution 2654, para 6.
32 ibid., para 3.
33 ibid., para 4.
34 ibid., paras 7 and 8.

After the vote, the USA's representative repeated his country's view of 'Morocco's autonomy plan as serious credible and realistic and one potential approach to satisfying [the] aspirations' of the people of Western Sahara as well as those of the inhabitants of the region.[35] However, it is recalled that, in the proclamation of 10 December 2020, recognising Morocco's sovereignty over Western Sahara, President Trump declared that the USA affirmed 'its support for Morocco's autonomy proposal as the only basis for a just and lasting solution to the dispute'.[36] Consequently, the observation that the adoption of Morocco's autonomy proposal provides one way in which the dispute might be settled is incompatible with the USA's official position, which has not been altered by the Biden administration in the intervening period.

Two non-permanent Council members, Gabon and the United Arab Emirates (UAE), also proclaimed their support for Morocco's autonomy initiative in the context of the adoption of Resolution 2654. In its statement, Gabon explained that it supported the UN process of finding 'a realistic, feasible and lasting political solution'.[37] Gabon's representative said that his country's vote reflected its 'support for Morocco's autonomy plan, which presents credible and reassuring prospects that allow not only for a way out of the current impasse but also for a mutually acceptable political solution to be reached'.[38] The UAE was more forthright in its endorsement of Morocco's position, offering its 'full support for the Kingdom of Morocco and its sovereignty over the entire Moroccan Sahara'.[39] As a result, the UAE's representative advocated in favour of Morocco's autonomy initiative, which 'is in line with the Charter of the United Nations and the Organization's resolutions and preserves Morocco's territorial integrity' in his country's opinion.[40] He also observed that the Council considers this proposal to be 'serious and credible' as apparent from its resolutions on this issue.[41]

The Kenyan representative explained that, in his country's view, Resolution 2654 did not 'substantively reflect the Security Council's commitment' to provide for the self-determination of the people of Western Sahara in a manner that is consistent with the UN Charter.[42] Kenya's main criticism was that there had been a 'gradual but noticeable shift away from [MINURSO's] mandate' over successive resolutions and it suggested that Resolution 2654 had continued this trend.[43] Kenya's representative noted

35 S/PV. 9168, p. 2.
36 See the discussion in Chapter V below.
37 S/PV. 9168, p. 5.
38 ibid.
39 ibid., 3.
40 ibid.
41 ibid.
42 ibid.
43 ibid.

that his country sought to encourage a return to the Mission's 'core objective of implementing a referendum for the self-determination of the people of Western Sahara'.[44] In this regard, it is worth noting that operative paragraph 2 of Resolution 2654 stressed 'the importance of aligning the strategic focus of MINURSO' with 'the need to achieve a realistic, practicable, enduring and mutually acceptable political solution [...] based on compromise', rather than the Mission's original purpose of organising and supporting a referendum of the Territory's inhabitants. Arguably, this paragraph amounts to an attempt to repurpose MINURSO in a way that accords with the view of the Moroccan government, ignoring the Mission's original purpose, and reducing it to a peace-keeping role. Russia, which abstained in response to Resolution 2654, delivered an assessment of the shortcomings of the Council's current approach to the Western Sahara Question which was very similar to those it has given in previous years.[45]

Russia, alone among the P5 membership, has been critical of the Council's shift away from the established formula for addressing the dispute. Moreover, the need to respect and implement the principles and procedures of decolonisation in this setting has been championed by several non-permanent members, such as South Africa and Kenya, over the years. However, the Council's implied acceptance of Morocco's autonomy plan, along with its recent emphasis on 'the need to make progress towards a realistic, practical and enduring political solution', has enabled sympathetic third States and IOs to endorse Morocco's autonomy proposal – which is premised on Morocco already exercising sovereignty over Western Sahara – while claiming to support the UN's peace process despite the autonomy proposal's incompatibility with international law. Undoubtedly, the Security Council has been prepared to accommodate Morocco's preferences, largely due to the support provided by certain P5 members.[46] Growing support for Morocco's autonomy plan in the Security Council has had the effect of shifting responsibility away from Morocco having to satisfy the established formula for settling the dispute along the lines agreed in the 1988 Settlement Proposals, and placing pressure on the Polisario to accept the territorial status quo as forming the basis for negotiations. It follows, therefore, that a 'mutually acceptable political solution' in this context means that the Polisario must accept the extant political reality rather than for both sides to change their positions to arrive at a genuine compromise arrangement.

44 ibid., 2.
45 ibid., 3–4.
46 See the discussion in Chapter V(A) below.

B. The General Assembly and Western Sahara in Recent Years

(i) C24 and Fourth Committee Meetings Since 2020

During the Fourth Committee's 2020 proceedings concerning the Western Sahara Question, participating States expressed divergent views about settling the Territory's final status.[47] Several States took the opportunity to make statements in support of the people of Western Sahara, their right to self-determination and the international community's responsibility to facilitate its exercise through the holding of a referendum in the Territory.[48] Conversely, a significant number of States endorsed Morocco's autonomy initiative as means of settling the conflict in this forum. They drew attention to the positive impact of Morocco's economic investment programmes, as far as its 'southern provinces' were concerned, while commending its concerted efforts to combat COVID-19 within the Sahel region. Such States were careful to express their support for the UN-sponsored political process while reiterating the novel language used in recent Council resolutions, which emphasised the need to achieve a realistic, practicable, and enduring political solution to the dispute based on compromise.[49] Some States went further by arguing that Morocco's autonomy initiative provides the way in which Morocco's territorial integrity and sovereignty over its 'Sahara region' can be respected.[50] However, certain States endorsed Morocco's claim to Western Sahara in more categorical terms. For example, the Comoros, Sao Tome and Principe, and Guinea-Bissau chose to refer explicitly to the 'Moroccan Sahara' when discussing Western Sahara and reporting that they had decided to open consulates in either Laayoune or Dakhla (in Moroccan-controlled Western Sahara) in recognition of the validity of Morocco's claim to the Territory.[51]

47 Due to the COVID-19 pandemic, the Fourth Committee instructed participating States to submit thematic statements rather than following a case-by-case approach.

48 These States included: Guyana and Belize, Fourth Committee, 6th meeting, 22 October 2020, A/C.4/75/SR.6, [28] and [62]; Ethiopia, Uganda and Lesotho, 7th meeting, 23 October 2020, A/C.4/75/SR.7, [40], [56] and [83]; Namibia, and Algeria, 8th meeting, 3 November 2020, A/C.4/75/SR.8, [10], and [85–88].

49 See, e.g., the statements made by Grenada and Gabon, Fourth Committee, 6th meeting, 22 October 2020, A/C.4/75/SR.6, [72] and [67]; Burkina Faso, 5th meeting, 20 October 2020, A/C.4/75/SR.5, [21]; Dominica, 7th meeting, 23 October 2020, A/C.4/75/SR.7, [52–53]; and Benin, 8th meeting, 3 November 2020, A/C.4/75/SR.8, [65].

50 These States included some of the signatories to the Laayoune Declaration, namely, Papua New Guinea, Fourth Committee, 3rd meeting, 15 October 2020, A/C.4/75/SR.3, [53], Kiribati, 7th meeting, 23 October 2020, A/C.4/75/SR.7, [72]. Other third countries have adopted the same stance, including El Salvador, 8th meeting, 3 November 2020, A/C.4/75/SR.8, [54].

51 See, e.g., the statement made by representatives of the Comoros, Fourth Committee, 7th meeting, 23 October 2020, A/C.4/75/SR.7, [58-60]; Sao Tome & Principe and Guinea-Bissau, 8th meeting, 3 November 2020, A/C.4/75/SR.8, [32] and [70]. Also, see Chapter V(B) below.

On 14 June 2021, the C24 considered the Western Sahara Question.[52] It is worth reflecting on Morocco's arguments on this issue before considering the countervailing positions of other States participating in the C24's 2021 meetings.[53] There was considerable divergence regarding the characterisation of the current situation and the applicable international law. State representatives tended either to offer strong support to Morocco's claim that Western Sahara is an integral part of its national territory, or they endorsed the Sahrawi people's right to self-determination, calling for its exercise through the holding of a referendum in accordance with the provisions of the Colonial Declaration (General Assembly Resolution 1514 (XV) of 14 December 1960), the UN Charter, and the UN's resolutions on Western Sahara.

On this occasion, Morocco's representative provided a restatement of Morocco's position as far as its claim to Western Sahara is concerned.[54] First, Morocco reasserted its claim that the 'Moroccan Sahara' was an integral part of its territory prior to the advent of Spanish colonialism.[55] It referred to the International Court of Justice's (ICJ's) findings in its 1975 *Western Sahara* Advisory Opinion, that (i) the Territory had not been *terra nullius* at the moment of Spanish colonisation; and (ii) pre-colonial legal ties of allegiance existed between the Saharan tribes and the Moroccan King.[56] Morocco's representative added that the current dispute about Western Sahara has nothing to do with decolonisation and should not be considered by the C24 or the Fourth Committee at all. Instead, he contended that it should be addressed exclusively by the Security Council.[57] However, the claim that the ICJ 'recognized the Moroccan character of the area' in its Advisory Opinion[58] is without foundation. Moreover, while Morocco referred to the ICJ's ruling that legal ties existed between Saharan tribes and Morocco during the pre-colonial era,[59] it ignored the Court's conclusion that because such ties did not manifest a sovereign nature, they did not confer title to the Territory on Morocco during that period. As discussed in Chapter 2(A)(ii), the ICJ confirmed that any rights that Morocco possessed in relation to Western Sahara were incapable of affecting the Territory's decolonisation in accordance with the provisions of Resolution 1514 (XV) (1960) and the principles contained in the UN Charter.[60]

Morocco's representative claimed that Western Sahara does not constitute a Non-Self-Governing Territory (NSGT) for the purpose of bringing about

52 A/AC.109/2021/17 (21 January 2021). See C24's 2021 Report, A/76/23, paras 96–100.

53 The Committee heard statements from interested organisations, individuals, and States.

54 Third Meeting of the C24, A/AC.109/2021/17 (14 June 2021).

55 ibid., para 14.

56 ibid.

57 ibid.

58 ibid.

59 ibid.

60 *Western Sahara* Advisory Opinion (1975) *ICJ Reps* 12, paras 59 and 162.

the process of decolonisation under the aegis of the General Assembly.[61] In this respect, Morocco's position appears to be underpinned by a conception of colonialism, which was formulated by the General Assembly for the task of identifying those principles that would determine whether a given territory qualified as a NSGT in relation to the reporting requirements contained in Article 73(e) of the UN Charter. In particular, Principle IV of Resolution 1541(XV) of 15 December 1960 stated that an obligation to transmit information exists 'in respect of a Territory which is geographically separate and distinct ethically and/or culturally from the country administering it'.[62] This formulation was devised in response to claims, made by several resistant colonial powers – notably Spain, Portugal, and France – that their overseas territories were municipal provinces rather than colonies, and thus they were not eligible to be classified as NSGTs. Consequently, the Assembly's definition of a NSGT focused on legitimate ways through which a distinction between the metropolitan State and an overseas territory could be drawn to show how colonial territories could qualify as NSGTs for reporting purposes, along with the associated obligations imposed on administering Powers by Chapter XI of the Charter.[63] This approach was underpinned by the idea that 'classical' colonialism is an overseas phenomenon. By implicitly harnessing this measure of colonialism, Morocco argued that Western Sahara 'is not geographically separate from Morocco'.[64] Moreover, in keeping with the ICJ's finding that pre-colonial ties existed across the Sahara region, Morocco contended that the Territory 'had the same tribal and ethnic groups, dialects, and culture as other parts of the country' as well as the same religion.[65] This statement can be read as a reference to Principle IV of Resolution 1541, in that it endeavours to show that the inhabitants of Western Sahara are not ethnically or culturally different from the Moroccan people. However, such an argument cannot overcome the General Assembly's decision to identify Western Sahara as a NSGT in 1963 or the ICJ's findings in its *Western Sahara* Advisory Opinion, as discussed in Chapter 2(A)(ii) above.

The UN's position remains that Western Sahara constitutes a NGST with Spain as its *de jure* administering power. Consequently, the C24 and Fourth Committee must continue to monitor developments in the Territory on that basis.[66] As discussed in Chapter 2(A)(iii), Morocco's argument is based on the

61 C24 Third Meeting, para 14.

62 Principle IV of General Assembly Resolution 1541 (XV) (15 December 1960).

63 For instance, Principle V of Resolution 1541 sets out the factors that would affect the relationship between the Metropolitan State and the territory concerned in such a way that the latter would be placed in a position of subordination.

64 C24 Third Meeting, para 14.

65 ibid.

66 In contrast, the EU Commission and Council have adopted the novel idea that Morocco performs the role of a *de facto* administering Power in relation to Western Sahara. In his 2018 Opinion in the *Western Sahara Campaign* Case, Advocate-General Wathelet observed that the notion of

assertion that Spain transferred its sovereign authority in respect of Western Sahara to Morocco by means of the Madrid Accords. It contended that the Accords were endorsed by the General Assembly via Resolution 3458B (XXX) (1975), thereby confirming that Western Sahara is an integral part of Morocco.[67] The Moroccan observer concluded his remarks by stating that his country remains involved in the UN political process concerning this dispute and he reminded the C24 that the Security Council considered Morocco's autonomy plan for the region to be both serious and credible.[68] He added that this proposal 'was the only possible basis for a realistic, pragmatic and lasting political solution [...] based on the sovereignty, territorial integrity and national unity of Morocco'.[69]

States supportive of Morocco's position vis-à-vis Western Sahara were careful to voice their support for the UN-sponsored process.[70] Nevertheless, they repeated the controversial phrases which have become a feature of Security Council resolutions on Western Sahara since 2018, in an effort to generate 'realistic' and 'pragmatic' outcomes that inevitably favour the Moroccan position since they assume that the territorial status quo forms the basis for any negotiations.[71] For instance, Ivory Coast sought to echo the Security Council's support for 'a realistic, pragmatic and lasting solution based on compromise' and Djibouti, Papua New Guinea, and Burkina Faso made very similar remarks.[72] Many States commended Morocco for its autonomy plan for the Western Sahara.[73] In so doing, they sought to arrogate the Council's language to bolster this 'serious and credible' proposal for settling

a *de facto* administering power is unknown to international law (Case 266/16, para 223). The CJEU found it unnecessary to examine this argument, which was advanced by the Commission and Council, as Morocco had always denied that it acted as an administering power in respect of the Territory. See Western Sahara Campaign judgment, para 72. Also, Stephen Allen, 'Exploiting Non-Self-Governing Territory Status: Western Sahara and the New EU/Morocco Sustainable Fisheries Partnership Agreement' (2020) 9(1) *CILJ* 24, 31–42.

67 This standpoint is implicit in its C24 statement (para 14).

68 C24 Third meeting, 14 June 2021, para 15.

69 ibid.

70 See, e.g., the statements made by Ivory Coast (2nd meeting, para 87); Antigua & Barbuda, (2nd meeting, para 93); Equatorial Guinea (3rd meeting, para 21); Saudi Arabia (3rd meeting, para 25), Djibouti (3rd meeting, para 27), Jordan (3rd meeting, para 28), Burkina Faso (3rd meeting, para 32), Burundi (3rd meeting, para 35), and the Comoros (3rd meeting, para 54).

71 See the discussion of the resolutions adopted by the Security Council on Western Sahara since 2018 in section A above.

72 Ivory Coast, C24, Second Meeting, para 87. Djibouti used the same language in its statement to the Committee, (C24, Third Meeting, para 27) as did Papua New Guinea in virtually the same terms (C24, Second Meeting, para 101) and Burkina Faso (3rd meeting, para 32).

73 E.g., see the statements made by Ivory Coast (2nd meeting, para 88), Dominica (2nd meeting, para 94), Saint Lucia (2nd meeting, para 97), Papua New Guinea (2nd meeting, para 101), Grenada, (3rd meeting, para 12), Gambia (3rd meeting, para 19), Equatorial Guinea (3rd meeting, para 21), Eswatini (3rd meeting, para 23), Saudi Arabia (3rd meeting, para 25), Djibouti (3rd meeting, para 27), Jordan (3rd meeting, para 28), Burkina Faso (3rd meeting, para 32), Burundi (3rd meeting,

the conflict.[74] Further, several States claimed that this initiative is consistent with international law and the UN's resolutions concerning the dispute.[75]

Some States stressed that the disputed Territory was an integral part of Morocco and that any settlement would need to respect Morocco's sovereignty and territorial integrity over its Sahara region.[76] As noted previously, certain States saw Morocco's conduct in relation to the Guerguerat crisis as legitimate action taken by a sovereign State within its national territory to protect its citizens and/or to maintain free movement across the Mauritanian border.[77] A number of States also praised Morocco for its peaceful efforts to uphold the ceasefire during this period.[78] Virtually all States favouring Morocco's position vis-à-vis Western Sahara applauded Morocco for its economic development of the 'Moroccan Sahara'; its declared efforts to improve the human rights of the region's inhabitants; and/or for its COVID-19 vaccination campaign both across 'its' territory and beyond.[79] These comments seem to reflect wider concerns in the Sahel region about investment, and key human rights indicators as well as stability and security considerations.

A considerable number of States pledged their support for the Sahrawi people's right to self-determination in keeping with the formulation devised by the ICJ, in its *Western Sahara* Advisory Opinion.[80] These States invariably proclaimed the pressing need to hold a referendum to guarantee the exercise of this entitlement, in accordance with the established modalities

---

para 35), Bahrain (3rd meeting, para 44), Gabon (3rd meeting, para 47) , UAE (3rd meeting, para 49), Senegal (3rd meeting, para 51), and the Comoros (3rd meeting, para 54).

74 E.g., see the statements made by Grenada, (3rd meeting, para 12), Eswatini (3rd meeting, para 23), Jordan (3rd meeting, para 28), Burkina Faso (3rd meeting, para 32), Bahrain (3rd meeting, para 44).

75 E.g., see the statements made by Ivory Coast (2nd meeting, para 88), Jordan (3rd meeting, para 28), Burundi (3rd meeting, para 35), Bahrain (3rd meeting, para 44), and Gabon (3rd meeting, para 47).

76 E.g., see the statements made by the Gambia (3rd meeting, para 19), Saudi Arabia (3rd meeting, para 26), Jordan (3rd meeting, para 28), Bahrain (3rd meeting, para 44), and UAE (3rd meeting, para 49).

77 E.g., see the statements made by Ivory Coast (2nd meeting, para 89), Grenada, (3rd meeting, para 13), Saudi Arabia (3rd meeting, para 26), Bahrain (3rd meeting, para 44), Gabon (3rd meeting, para 48), Senegal (3rd meeting, para 52), and the Comoros (3rd meeting, para 55).

78 E.g., see the statements made by Papua New Guinea (2nd meeting, para 101), Grenada, (3rd meeting, para 13), Saudi Arabia (3rd meeting, para 26), Gabon (3rd meeting, para 48), and the Comoros (3rd meeting, para 55).

79 E.g., see the statements made by Ivory Coast (2nd meeting, para 88), Antigua & Barbuda (2nd meeting, para 93), Dominica (2nd meeting, para 95), Saint Lucia (2nd meeting, para 97), the Gambia (3rd meeting, para 19), Equatorial Guinea (3rd meeting, para 21), Eswatini (3rd meeting, para 23), Saudi Arabia (3rd meeting, para 26), Djibouti (3rd meeting, para 27), Jordan (3rd meeting, para 28), Burkina Faso (3rd meeting, para 33), Burundi (3rd meeting, para 36), Gabon (3rd meeting, para 48) , UAE (3rd meeting, para 50), Senegal (3rd meeting, para 52), and the Comoros (3rd meeting, para 54).

80 *Western Sahara* Advisory Opinion, para 59.

of decolonisation,[81] and in a manner consistent with the UN Charter and the Organisation's resolutions on Western Sahara.[82] Nevertheless, States coming within this group were mindful to offer their support to the UN's search for a negotiated solution to the dispute.[83] Many States in this group insisted that the dispute concerning Western Sahara's status is about decolonisation by reference to the applicable law.[84] In addition, they implored the C24 to take decisive action to ensure that the UN satisfies its obligation to deliver self-determination for the people of Western Sahara.[85] The strongest criticism of Morocco's conduct came from South Africa, Namibia, and Algeria. South Africa accused 'the occupying Power' of violating the ceasefire agreement which precipitated the resumption of hostilities.[86] It added that: 'Any recognition of Western Sahara as a part of Morocco was a contravention of international law, as it was tantamount to the recognition of [an] illegal occupation'.[87] Namibia 'called on the occupying Power to end its occupation and stop undermining the territorial integrity of Western Sahara'.[88] The Algerian representative pointed to Morocco's deliberate obstruction of the arrangements required for the holding of a referendum. He observed there have been 'too many hampered initiatives' over the last three decades, during which time the Sahrawi people have suffered serious human rights violations alongside the unlawful exploitation of their natural resources.[89]

81 See discussion in Chapter II(A)(iii) above.

82 See, e.g., the statements made by Cuba (2nd meeting, para 91), Nicaragua (3rd meeting, para 1), Timor-Leste (3rd meeting, para 2), Ecuador (3rd meeting, para 6), Venezuela (3rd meeting, para 7), Zimbabwe (3rd meeting, para 20), Mozambique (3rd meeting, para 24), South Africa (3rd meeting, paras 29–31), Namibia (3rd meeting, para 34), Botswana (3rd meeting, para 37), Angola (3rd meeting, para 39), Algeria (3rd meeting, paras 40–41), Lesotho (3rd meeting, paras 45–46), and Iran (3rd meeting, para 57).

83 See, e.g., the statements made by Cuba (2nd meeting, para 91), Nicaragua (3rd meeting, para 1), Timor-Leste (3rd meeting, para 2), Ecuador (3rd meeting, para 6), Venezuela (3rd meeting, para 8), Zimbabwe (3rd meeting, para 20), Mozambique (3rd meeting, para 24), South Africa (3rd meeting, para 31), Namibia (3rd meeting, para 34), Botswana (3rd meeting, para 37), Angola (3rd meeting, para 39), Algeria (3rd meeting, paras 42–43), Lesotho (3rd meeting, para 46), and Iran (3rd meeting, para 57).

84 See, e.g., the statements made by Venezuela (3rd meeting, para 7), Botswana (3rd meeting, paras 37–38), Angola (3rd meeting, para 39), and Algeria (3rd meeting, para 40).

85 See, e.g., the statement contained in the preamble to GAR 75/106 (2020). See, e.g., the statements Venezuela (3rd meeting, para 9,), South Africa (3rd meeting, para 31), Namibia (3rd meeting, para 34), and Algeria (3rd meeting, para 42). Some representatives urged the C24 to organise a new visiting mission to Western Sahara. See the statements made by Timor-Leste (3rd meeting, para 4), Zimbabwe (3rd meeting, para 20), South Africa (3rd meeting, para 31), Botswana (3rd meeting, para 38), and Lesotho (3rd meeting, para 46).

86 South Africa (3rd meeting, para 29).

87 ibid., para 31.

88 Namibia (3rd meeting, para 34).

89 Algeria (3rd meeting, para 41).

During the Fourth Committee's plenary sessions in 2021, South Africa, Timor-Leste, Algeria, and Namibia reiterated the key arguments they made earlier in the C24's proceedings.[90] In addition, South Africa reminded the Fourth Committee of its responsibility to assist the Sahrawi people in their efforts to exercise their inalienable right to self-determination by means of holding the UN-mandated referendum.[91] Timor-Leste drew attention to the serious challenges posed by the resumption of hostilities;[92] and Algeria warned against any attempt to re-characterise the Western Sahara Question as being about anything other than decolonisation.[93]

Forty-seven statements were made by States participating in the 2022 meetings dedicated to the Western Sahara Question in the C24.[94] The overwhelming majority of such States strenuously supported either Morocco's position or the Polisario's cause. That said, more States were willing to endorse Morocco's autonomy initiative than in previous years, and the support offered, by certain States, for Morocco's sovereignty claim was arguably more vociferous, too. This development was not lost on the States involved, with Papua New Guinea and Gabon both commenting on the increasing support shown for Morocco's autonomy plan by the international community.[95] Many sympathetic States reiterated their support for Morocco's autonomy plan on this occasion, often accompanied by the observation that it represents a 'serious and credible' plan, as appreciated by the Security Council, which is 'realistic' and 'consistent with international law'.[96] In pledging their support, several States explicitly connected the autonomy initiative to the maintenance

90 See South Africa's statement to the Fourth Committee (9th plenary meeting 20 October 2021); Timor-Leste's statement to the Fourth Committee (9th plenary meeting 20 October 2021); Algeria's statement to the Fourth Committee (11th plenary meeting 25 October 2021); and Namibia's statement to the Fourth Committee (12th plenary meeting 27 October 2021).

91 South Africa's statement to the Fourth Committee (9th plenary meeting 20 October 2021), p. 2.

92 Timor-Leste's statement to the Fourth Committee (9th plenary meeting 20 October 2021), p. 3.

93 Algeria's statement to the Fourth Committee (11th plenary meeting 25 October 2021), p. 2.

94 Several statements were also made by individuals and organisations during these sessions. See A/AC.109/2022/SR.3 and SR.4 (13 June 2022).

95 C24 2022, 4th meeting, para 8. Gabon commented on the existence of considerable international support for this plan during the same session (C24 2022, 4th meeting, para 9).

96 E.g., see statement made by Ivory Coast (C24 2022, 3rd meeting, para 81); Grenada (C24 2022, 3rd meeting, para 84); Sierra Leone (C24 2022, 3rd meeting, para 86); Antigua (C24 2022, 3rd meeting, para 90); Guatemala (C24 2022, 3rd meeting, para 92); Dominica (C24 2022, 4th meeting, para 4); St Lucia (C24 2022, 4th meeting, para 5), Papua New Guinea (C24 2022, 4th meeting, para 8); Gabon (C24 2022, 4th meeting, para 9); Bahrain (C24 2022, 4th meeting, para 12); Senegal (C24 2022, 4th meeting, para 14); Jordan (C24 2022, 4th meeting, para 15); Saudi Arabia (C24 2022, 4th meeting, para 16); Benin (C24 2022, 4th meeting, para 17); Equatorial Guinea (C24 2022, 4th meeting, para 18); Burkina Faso (C24 2022, 4th meeting, para 20); Gambia (C24 2022, 4th meeting, para 22); Djibouti (C24 2022, 4th meeting, para 23); Qatar (C24 2022, 4th meeting, para 26); UAE (C24 2022, 4th meeting, para 27); Guinea-Bissau (C24 2022, 4th meeting, para 30); Kuwait (C24 2022, 4th meeting, para 36); Liberia (C24 2022, 4th meeting, para 34); and Comoros (C24 2022, 4th meeting, para 39).

and protection of Morocco's territorial integrity and the exercise of sovereignty over the 'Moroccan Sahara'.[97]

Certain States renewed their praise for Morocco's development and investment strategy for its 'southern provinces',[98] which has had a positive effect on the region's human rights index, they claimed.[99] Some States applauded Morocco for the elections that it held in Western Sahara on 8 September 2021, claiming that this amounted to an exercise in democracy which 'enabled the local population to choose its representatives freely'.[100] Many sympathetic States also commended the Moroccan government for its regional COVID-19 vaccination campaign.[101] Finally, a few States chose to congratulate Morocco for its restraint since the resumption of hostilities and its efforts to uphold the ceasefire.[102]

Despite the discernible shift in favour of Morocco's position, many participating States expressed their support for the exercise of the right to self-determination by the people of Western Sahara in keeping with the terms of

97 E.g., see the statement made by Guatemala (C24 2022, 3rd meeting, para 92); Dominica (C24 2022, 4th meeting, para 4); Gabon (C24 2022, 4th meeting, para 9); Bahrain (C24 2022, 4th meeting, para 12); Senegal (C24 2022, 4th meeting, para 14); Jordan (C24 2022, 4th meeting, para 15); Saudi Arabia (C24 2022, 4th meeting, para 16); Equatorial Guinea (C24 2022, 4th meeting, para 18); Gambia (C24 2022, 4th meeting, para 22); Qatar (C24 2022, 4th meeting, para 26); UAE (C24 2022, 4th meeting, para 27); Yemen UAE (C24 2022, 4th meeting, para 33); Kuwait (C24 2022, 4th meeting, para 36); Liberia (C24 2022, 4th meeting, para 34); and Comoros (C24 2022, 4th meeting, para 39).

98 E.g., Dominica (C24 2022, 4th meeting), para 4.

99 E.g., see statement made by Ivory Coast (C24 2022, 3rd meeting, para 81). Also see the positive comments made by Sierra Leone (C24 2022, 3rd meeting, para 86); Papua New Guinea (C24 2022, 4th meeting, para 8); Jordan (C24 2022, 4th meeting, para 15); Saudi Arabia (C24 2022, 4th meeting, para 16); Benin (C24 2022, 4th meeting, para 17); Gambia (C24 2022, 4th meeting, para 22); Qatar (C24 2022, 4th meeting, para 26); UAE (C24 2022, 4th meeting, para 27); Guinea-Bissau (C24 2022, 4th meeting, para 30); Sao Tome and Principe (C24 2022, 4th meeting, para 35); and Comoros (C24 2022, 4th meeting, para 39).

100 Statement made by Ivory Coast (C24 2022, 3rd meeting, para 81). Also see Papua New Guinea (C24 2022, 4th meeting, para 8); Gabon (C24 2022, 4th meeting, para 9); Senegal (C24 2022, 4th meeting, para 14); Saudi Arabia (C24 2022, 4th meeting, para 16); Djibouti (C24 2022, 4th meeting, para 23); Guinea-Bissau (C24 2022, 4th meeting, para 30); Liberia (C24 2022, 4th meeting, para 34); and Comoros (C24 2022, 4th meeting, para 39). On this point, Morocco's observer claimed that the population of the 'Moroccan Sahara' enjoyed 'the highest rates of political participation of any region of Morocco, as had been confirmed in the recent elections of 8 September 2021, which has seen a turnout of 63%', C24 2022, 4th meeting, para 41.

101 E.g., see statement made by Ivory Coast (C24 2022, 3rd meeting, para 81); Sierra Leone (C24 2022, 3rd meeting, para 86); Papua New Guinea (C24 2022, 4th meeting, para 8); Jordan (C24 2022, 4th meeting, para 15); Saudi Arabia (C24 2022, 4th meeting, para 16); Gambia (C24 2022, 4th meeting, para 22); UAE (C24 2022, 4th meeting, para 27); and Guinea-Bissau (C24 2022, 4th meeting, para 30).

102 E.g., see statement made by Ivory Coast (C24 2022, 3rd meeting, para 81); Antigua (C24 2022, 3rd meeting, para 90); Gabon (C24 2022, 4th meeting, para 9); Saudi Arabia (C24 2022, 4th meeting, para 16); Djibouti (C24 2022, 4th meeting, para 23); and Comoros (C24 2022, 4th meeting, para 39).

the Colonial Declaration, the UN Charter, and the international law relating to decolonisation.[103] A number of these States called for the holding of a referendum involving only the people of Western Sahara leading to the achievement of independence.[104] Several States adopted an overtly critical stance regarding Morocco's conduct vis-à-vis Western Sahara.[105] Botswana's representative expressed his country's 'solidarity with the people of Western Sahara' while regretting the lack of progress on resolving this dispute which he attributed to 'unilateral obstruction' which 'had caused the collapse of the 1991 ceasefire in November 2020 and the ensuing escalation of military hostilities'.[106] South Africa's representative insisted that Morocco's autonomy plan 'was unilateral and had no basis in international law' [since] it assumed that Western Sahara was part of Morocco'.[107] Algeria's representative was also strongly critical of Morocco's plan. He contended that:

> The so called "autonomy" initiative was no more than an effort by Morocco to [...] continue to plunder the Sahrawi people's resources. States that supported that initiative were complicit in the hegemonic attempt by Morocco to impose its sovereignty on territory outside its internationally recognized boundaries. The initiative or any other option that did not allow the Sahrawi people to exercise their inalienable rights through a free and fair referendum was contrary to international law [...].[108]

Morocco's representative attempted to close this issue by reminding the C24 that it remained engaged in the UN political process concerning the resolution of this 'regional dispute' essentially between itself and Algeria with the Polisario acting as the latter's proxy in this regard. However, he noted that the 'realistic, pragmatic and credible [...] solution [...] was in fact embodied in the Moroccan autonomy plan in the context of the sovereignty and territorial

103 E.g., see the statements made by Venezuela (C24 2022, 3rd meeting, para 78); Cuba (C24 2022, 3rd meeting, para 82); Nicaragua (C24 2022, 3rd meeting, para 83); Iran (C24 2022, 4th meeting, para 3); Bolivia (C24 2022, 4th meeting, para 6); Ecuador (C24 2022, 4th meeting, para 7); Botswana (C24 2022, 4th meeting, para 11); Angola (C24 2022, 4th meeting, para 13); South Africa (C24 2022, 4th meeting, para 19); Namibia (C24 2022, 4th meeting, para 21); Paraguay (C24 2022, 4th meeting, para 24); Mexico (C24 2022, 4th meeting, para 28); Algeria (C24 2022, 4th meeting, para 31); and Zimbabwe (C24 2022, 4th meeting, para 34).

104 E.g., see the statements made by Venezuela (C24 2022, 3rd meeting, para 78); Timor-Leste (C24 2022, 3rd meeting, para 87); Iran (C24 2022, 4th meeting, para 3); Botswana (C24 2022, 4th meeting, para 11); Angola (C24 2022, 4th meeting, para 13); South Africa (C24 2022, 4th meeting, para 19); Mexico (C24 2022, 4th meeting, para 28); Algeria (C24 2022, 4th meeting, para 32); and Zimbabwe (C24 2022, 4th meeting, para 34).

105 Botswana (C24 2022, 4th meeting, para 11); South Africa (C24 2022, 4th meeting, para 19); and Algeria (C24 2022, 4th meeting, paras 31–32).

106 Botswana (C24 2022, 4th meeting, para 11).

107 South Africa (C24 2022, 4th meeting, para 19).

108 Algeria (C24 2022, 4th meeting, para 32).

integrity of Morocco'.[109] He went on to claim that the plan was 'gaining [...] international support' as apparent from statements made during the present proceedings and elsewhere.[110]

Certain States which participated in the C24's 2022 meetings on Western Sahara reinforced their positions by submitting statements to the Fourth Committee in that year.[111] Other States, which had not participated in the C24's meetings on Western Sahara in 2022, took the opportunity to address this dispute by making submissions to the Fourth Committee. For example, Mozambique strenuously expressed its commitment to the task of 'finding the acceptable solution to allow the people of Western Sahara to exercise their inalienable right to self-determination, in accordance with [...] General Assembly Resolution 1514'.[112] In its statement, Cabo Verde, which has recently opened a consulate in occupied Western Sahara,[113] pledged its support for the UN-sponsored political process concerning Western Sahara while declaring its commitment to the upholding of the right to self-determination contained in Resolution 1514. Nevertheless, Cabo Verde incongruously chose to endorse Morocco's autonomy initiative 'as the only basis for a just and lasting political settlement of this long-running regional dispute'.[114]

(ii) Recent General Assembly Resolutions on Western Sahara

On 10 December 2020, the General Assembly adopted Resolution 75/106 on the Western Sahara Question.[115] In the resolution's first preambular paragraph, the Assembly reaffirmed the inalienable right of all peoples to self-determination and independence in keeping with the principles contained in the UN Charter and the Colonial Declaration. It went on to acknowledge the full range of modalities by which this entitlement could be exercised, on the proviso that the outcome was the product of the freely expressed will of the people concerned.[116] The Assembly aligned itself with the Security Council's

109 C24 2022, 4th meeting, para 40. The Moroccan representative delivered the last statement on this agenda item although it was followed by a bad-tempered exchange with the Algerian representative (C24 2022, 4th meeting, paras 43–46).

110 The Moroccan observer claimed that the autonomy plan's supporters include 'Germany, Hungary, the Netherlands, the Philippines, Romania, Serbia, and Spain': C24 2022, 4th meeting, para 40. See further the discussion in Chapter V(A) below.

111 For example, see the statements delivered by Iran during the Second Plenary Meeting (3 October 2022); South Africa during the Seventh Plenary Meeting (11 October 2022); Namibia at the Eighth Plenary Meeting (13 October 2022); Sierra Leone during the Ninth Plenary Meeting held on 14 October 2022.

112 Eighth Plenary Meeting (13 October 2022).

113 Secretary-General's 2022 Report on Western Sahara, para 18.

114 Ninth Plenary Meeting (14 October 2022).

115 A/RES/75/106 (10 December 2020).

116 Resolution 75/106, Preamble, (para 2).

approach by identifying those resolutions which had established, and elaborated, the current negotiating framework.[117] It also chose to express its satisfaction with the negotiations previously undertaken by the parties.[118] In the resolution's operative paragraphs, the Assembly reaffirmed its support for the existing negotiating framework, 'with a view to achieving a just, lasting and mutually acceptable political solution, which will provide for the self-determination of the people of Western Sahara'.[119] It then, '[w]elcome[d] the commitment of the parties to continue to show political will and work in an atmosphere propitious for dialogue, in order to enter into a more intensive phase of negotiations, in good faith and without preconditions'.[120]

The Assembly lent its weight to the Council's approach to resolving this protracted dispute in Resolution 75/106, but it is notable that in recent years the Assembly's resolutions have only done so in general terms.[121] It has followed a practice of listing all the Council's resolutions on Western Sahara since 2007 without alluding to any substantive changes that have been made to the text of those resolutions over time.[122] In this respect, the Assembly may be trying to steer clear of the controversies generated by the Council's introduction of policy changes on Western Sahara since 2018 in an effort to avoid being closely associated with any developments that would frame the dispute as anything other than a frustrated case of decolonisation.

Despite the increasing support for Morocco's sovereignty claim to Western Sahara, and the growing number of States prepared to support Morocco's claim, either directly or indirectly, during meetings of the C24 and the Fourth Committee in 2021, the General Assembly adopted Resolution 76/89 on the Western Sahara Question on 9 December 2021, in essentially the same terms as Resolution 75/106. This trend continued during the General Assembly's 77th session. The draft resolution which was circulated for consideration during Fourth Committee proceedings on 10 October 2022 was virtually identical to its immediate predecessor. It was subsequently adopted by the Assembly, without amendment, as Resolution 77/133 on 15 December 2022. However, it is conceivable that the significant shift in favour of Morocco's position which seems to have been prompted by the resumption of hostilities may put the Assembly under pressure to re-evaluate the content of its resolutions on the Western Sahara Question in years to come.

117 i.e., from SCR 1754 (2007) to SCR 2494 (2019).

118 Resolution 75/106, para 4.

119 ibid., para 2.

120 ibid., para 3.

121 See, e.g., Resolution 74/97 (13 December 2019), Resolution 73/107 (7 December 2018), and Resolution 72/95 (7 December 2017).

122 See Chapter IV above.

5 Implications of Growing Support for the Moroccan Position on Western Sahara

A. Growing Support for the Moroccan Autonomy Plan: Has a Tipping Point Been Reached?

The modern political context surrounding expressions of support by third States for the Moroccan position is so dynamic that it can be difficult to keep track of current developments. For instance, on 14 September 2022, the day after his inauguration as President of Kenya, and following receipt of a 'congratulatory message' from King Mohammed VI of Morocco, William Ruto tweeted: 'Kenya rescinds its recognition of the Sahrawi Arab Democratic Republic (SADR) and initiates steps to wind down the entity's presence in the country'.[1] The tweet was deleted later the same day, and was followed by a 16 September 2022 note, circulated to embassies by the Principal Secretary of the Ministry of Foreign Affairs, reaffirming Kenya's long-standing support for the self-determination of the Sahrawi people, and its alignment with the decision of the Organisation of African Unity (OAU) to admit the SADR as a member in 1982, and with the subsequent approach of the African Union (AU) regarding the SADR.[2]

As discussed in Chapter 4(A) above, a more significant development is the USA's new approach of supporting the autonomy plan and recognising Morocco's annexation of Western Sahara. This was one of the last foreign policy acts of the Trump administration, and as was noted in the previous chapter, the new position has since been asserted by the US representative in the Security Council.[3] In short, the White House declared at the end of 2020 that '[t]he United States believes that an independent Sahrawi state is not a realistic option for resolving the conflict and that genuine autonomy

1 'Sahrawi Gaffe Hands Kenya's Ruto First Diplomatic Dilemma' *The East African* (16 September 2022) <https://www.theeastafrican.co.ke/tea/news/east-africa/sahrawi-gaffe-hands-kenya-ruto-first-diplomatic-dilemma-3950592> accessed 31 August 2023.

2 <https://www.the-star.co.ke/news/2022-09-18-kenya-clarifies-stand-on-sahrawi-republic-after-rutos-controversial-tweet/> accessed 31 August 2023. See also, 'Kenya Clarifies Position on Sahrawi After Gaffe' *The East African* (19 September 2022) <https://www.theeastafrican.co.ke/tea/news/east-africa/kenya-position-on-sahrawi-3953354> accessed 31 August 2023.

3 See the discussion in Chapter IV above.

DOI: 10.4324/9781032658827-5

under Moroccan sovereignty is the only feasible solution', and it endorsed Morocco's autonomy plan 'as the only framework to negotiate a mutually acceptable solution'.[4] This controversial policy shift away from the USA's formally neutral stance on the Western Sahara Question occurred as part of a package deal by which Washington recognised Morocco's claim to Western Sahara in return for Rabat's undertaking to start the process of resuming normal diplomatic relations with Israel.[5] The Biden administration has reportedly informed the Moroccan government of its decision not to reverse the policy 'for now', although it has been reluctant to make any official pronouncement to that effect.[6]

In a further important escalation, Morocco recalled its ambassadors from Berlin and Madrid in May 2021, requesting that both States 'clarify' their positions on Western Sahara. Germany did so, referring to the plan as 'serious and credible', and in a move that proved both surprising and controversial domestically, the Prime Minister of Spain – still nominally the *de jure* Administering Power in Western Sahara[7] – wrote to King Mohamed VI on 14 March 2022 with an even stronger endorsement.[8]

The Spanish letter – which only came to light after it was made public by the Moroccan authorities – speaks of establishing a 'new relationship' between the two countries, recognises the importance of the Western Sahara

4 'Israel-Morocco Agree to Normalise Relations in US Brokered Deal' *Al-Jazeera* (10 December 2020) <https://www.aljazeera.com/news/2020/12/10/israel-morocco-agree-to-normalise-relations-in-us-brokered-deal> accessed 31 August 2023 For a reaction that views this development through the prism of the international legal duty of non-recognition, see JA González Vega, 'El Reconocimiento por EE.UU de la Anexión Marroquí del Sáhara Occidental en Perspectiva: Aspectos Jurídicos y Políticos', 41 REEI (2021) <https://dialnet.unirioja.es/servlet/articulo?codigo=7983230> accessed 31 August 2023.

5 See 'United States Recognizes Morocco's Sovereignty Over Western Sahara' (2021) 115 *AJIL* 318–323.

6 It was reported that Secretary of State Anthony Blinken informed the Moroccan Minister in a telephone call that the Biden administration would not be reverse the policy 'for now', although this assurance was not recorded in the official read-out of the call: B Ravid, 'Biden won't reverse Trump's Western Sahara move, U.S. tells Morocco', *Axios* (30 April 2021): <https://www.axios.com/2021/04/30/biden-keep-trump-western-sahara-recogntion-morocco> accessed 31 August 2023; Moroccan state media, while taking comfort from the fact that Biden's spending Bill omitted the usual reference to 'Western Sahara', has characterised the Biden administration's affirmations of support for Morocco as 'tepid': S Kasroui, 'Western Sahara: US Support for Morocco's Position on Full Display in Latest Spending Bill' (16 March 2022): <https://www.moroccoworldnews.com/2022/03/347703/western-sahara-us-support-for-moroccos-position-on-full-display-in-latest-spending-bill> accessed 31 August 2023.

7 On this point, see the sources collected in C. Ruiz Miguel, M. Ponce de León Iglesias, and Y. Blanco Souto *El Sáhara Occidental: Prontuario Jurídico – 15 Enunciados Básicos Sobre el Conflicto* (2nd ed, Santiago de Compostela: Andavira 2019) Ch.10.

8 A copy of the original letter is at: <https://elpais.com/espana/2022-03-23/la-carta-de-pedro-sanchez-a-mohamed-vi-debemos-construir-una-nueva-relacion-que-evite-futuras-crisis.html> accessed 31 August 2023.

issue to Morocco and Morocco's 'serious and credible' efforts to find a mutually acceptable solution within the UN framework, and – crucially – recognises Morocco's 2007 autonomy plan as 'the most serious, credible and realistic basis for the resolution of the dispute'.[9] As discussed in Chapter 2(A)(iii), the importance of the new Spanish position was underscored by the Secretary-General in his 2022 Report on Western Sahara.

There has been speculation that Spain's change of policy was linked to Morocco stoking the migration crisis at the borders of Spain's North African enclaves of Ceuta and Melilla,[10] or even the hacking of the communications of the Spanish Prime Minister and other government Ministers whose portfolios covered relations with Morocco, using Pegasus spyware.[11] The speculation has been fuelled by the fact that the reversal of Spain's long-standing policy on Western Sahara has no obvious strategic rationale, as noted by Alejandro del Valle, who also draws attention to the irregular and opaque nature of the Spanish government's actions in this regard. He observes, for instance, that there was no mention of the change of policy in a document setting out the government's foreign policy strategy for 2021–24 that had been published less than a year earlier; that there was no prior consultation with the legislature or opposition; and that the government had initially (and bizarrely) maintained that there had been no change in the official Spanish position, before

9 ibid.

10 Interview with *El Pais* journalist Miguel González: <https://elpais.com/espana/2022-03-27/video-que-hay-detras-de-la-carta-de-pedro-sanchez-a-mohamed-vi.html> (27 March 2022) accessed 31 August 2023. <https://www.moroccoworldnews.com/2022/03/347810/western-sahara-france-reiterates-support-for-moroccos-autonomy-plan> (21 March 2022) accessed 31 August 2023. A low point came on 24 June 2022, with a horrific incident resulting in the deaths of 24 migrants, who were compelled by the Moroccan authorities to leave their makeshift camps and scale the heavily fortified border fence in Melilla. See the report of *BBC Africa Eye*, 1 November 2022: <https://www.bbc.co.uk/programmes/p0dbnttd> accessed 31 August 2023.

11 J Verdú, 'Corrupción en España, Europa y Sáhara Occidental' <https://www.europasur.es/opinion/articulos/Corrupcion-Europa-Espana-Sahara-Occidental_0_1758424199.html> (19 January 2023) accessed 31 August 2023. It has also been reported in the Spanish press that the Spanish Prime Minister fired the Foreign Minister, Arancha González Laya, at Morocco's behest, a week after a secret meeting on 2 July 2021. Morocco apparently insisted on the dismissal of González Laya as a precondition of dialogue aimed at normalising relations between the two countries: 'Sánchez cesó a González Laya como ministra una semana después de que Marruecos se lo pidiera' *El Confidencial* (19 April 2023). The secret meeting took place following a decision by Spain to admit the leader of the Polisario, Brahim Ghali, into the country under a pseudonym, so that he could receive treatment for COVID-19 in a Spanish hospital. The decision prompted Morocco to summon the Spanish ambassador and accuse Spain of acting in a manner that was 'inconsistent with the spirit of partnership and good neighbourliness': *Al Jazeera* 'Morocco scolds Spain over virus help for independence leader' (25 April 2021).

eventually admitting that there had indeed been a change of policy driven by the need to improve relations with Morocco.[12]

It was reported by *El País* that in the days leading up to the Spanish Prime Minister's letter, there were intense negotiations regarding the strength of Spain's endorsement of the Moroccan autonomy plan. It appears that a short time before the letter was sent, the wording was changed from 'a' to '*the most*' serious, credible, etc basis for a resolution of the dispute.[13] A few days later, after France had reiterated its support for the Moroccan autonomy plan as 'a serious and credible basis' for resolving the dispute, Moroccan state-sponsored media took the opportunity to highlight the significance of the strengthened Spanish wording, recalling that the Spanish government had endorsed the autonomy plan 'as the "most" credible and efficient solution to end the conflict over Western Sahara'.[14]

Such developments could come to be seen as a tipping point for the future of Western Sahara. Perhaps the most interesting recent development in State practice, reflecting the snowballing of support for Moroccan designs on Western Sahara, is the nascent practice of establishing consulates in the Territory. The next section examines this practice and its possible legal ramifications.

B. Establishing Consulates in Western Sahara and Implied Recognition

In his recent Reports on Western Sahara, the UN Secretary-General has drawn attention to Morocco's new strategy of encouraging sympathetic States to open consulates in the Territory.[15] For instance, in his October 2019 Report, he noted the first tentative step in this direction with Ivory Coast's inauguration of an honorary consulate in the city of Laayoune in Western Sahara on 26 June 2019.[16] In his next Report, the Secretary-General observed that, between 18 December 2019 and 12 March 2020, a number of African States had opened Consulates-General in either Laayoune or Dakhla, namely: Burundi, Central

12 Alejandro del Valle Gálvez, 'Ceuta, Melilla, Gibraltar y el Sáhara Occidental: Estrategias Españolas y Europeas para las Ciudades de Frontera Exterior en Africa, y los Peñones de Vélez y Alhucemas' (2022) 10 *Paix&SecIntl* 1, 10–13.

13 Interview with *El Pais* journalist Miguel González (27 March 2022): <https://elpais.com/espana/2022-03-27/video-que-hay-detras-de-la-carta-de-pedro-sanchez-a-mohamed-vi.html> accessed 31 August 2023.

14 <https://www.moroccoworldnews.com/2022/03/347810/western-sahara-france-reiterates-support-for-moroccos-autonomy-plan> (21 March 2022) accessed 31 August 2023.

15 Also see International Crisis Group, 'Time for International Re-Engagement in Western Sahara', Briefing No. 82, 11 March 2021.

16 Report on the situation in Western Sahara, S/2019/787 (2 October 2019) para 11. Morocco drew attention to this development during the Fourth Committee's session concerning Western Sahara on 16 October 2019. A/C.4/74/SR.8, para 57.

African Republic, Comoros, Djibouti, Gabon, Gambia, Guinea, Ivory Coast, Liberia, and São Tomé and Príncipe.[17] The trend of inaugurating Consulates-General in either Laayoune or Dakhla continued and began to include Middle Eastern States, too. Between September 2020 and the end of August 2021, the following States had either opened consulates in Western Sahara or announced their intention to do so: Bahrain, Burkina Faso, Equatorial Guinea, Eswatini, Guinea-Bissau, Haiti, Jordan, Libya, Malawi, Senegal, Sierra Leone, Suriname, the United Arab Emirates (UAE), and Zambia.[18] The Secretary-General added that, on 10 December 2020, the USA had issued a presidential proclamation stating that it recognised, 'Moroccan sovereignty over the entire Western Sahara territory',[19] followed by an announcement that it would inaugurate a 'virtual presence post for Western Sahara'.[20] In his 2022 Report, the Secretary-General observed that the Organisation of Eastern Caribbean States along with Suriname, Togo, and Cabo Verde had all inaugurated 'Consulates-General' in Dakhla in Western Sahara in 2022.[21]

It is necessary to consider the ramifications of these developments for the doctrine of recognition, and its application in the context of Morocco's claim to Western Sahara in particular. Consular relations are premised on the existence of mutual consent, which may be implied from the consent given to establish diplomatic relations.[22] However, it does not necessarily follow from the opening and running of a consulate in a disputed territory, claimed and controlled by the receiving State, that the sending State has recognised such a territorial claim. Article 4(2) of the Vienna Convention on Consular Relations (VCCR) provides that: 'A consular post, its classification, and the consular district shall be established by the sending State and shall be subject to the

17 The Secretary-General's 2020 Report on the Situation in Western Sahara, S/2020/938 (23 September 2020) para 6. On 12 March 2020, Ivory Coast opened a Consulate-General in Dakhla adding to its honorary consulate in Laayoune on 26 June 2019, as mentioned above.

18 Secretary-General's Report on the situation in Western Sahara, S/2021/843 (1 October 2021) para 17.

19 Report on the situation in Western Sahara, S/2021/843 (1 October 2021) para 18. For the full text see: 'Proclamation on Recognizing The Sovereignty Of The Kingdom Of Morocco Over The Western Sahara' – The White House (archives.gov) accessed 31 August 2023.

20 Report on the situation in Western Sahara, S/2021/843 (1 October 2021) para 18.

21 Report on the situation in Western Sahara, S/2022/733 (3 October 2022) para 18.

22 Article 2(1) and (2) Vienna Convention on Consular Relations (VCCR), (1963) 596 UNTS 261. The close connection between consular and diplomatic relations is apparent from Article 3 VCCR, which provides that consular functions are exercisable by both consular and diplomatic missions. Similarly, Article 3(2) of the Vienna Convention on Diplomatic Relations (VCDR) (1961) 500 UNTS 95 provides that: 'Nothing in the present Convention shall be construed as preventing the performance of consular functions by a diplomatic mission'. See Eileen Denza, *Diplomatic Law: Commentary on the Vienna Convention on Diplomatic Relations* (4th ed, OUP 2016) 31–33.

approval of the receiving State'.[23] Article 10 adds that: 'Heads of consular posts are appointed by the sending State and are admitted to the exercise of their functions by the receiving State'. The key consular functions are set out in Article 5(a)–(m), they include:

(a) protecting in the receiving State the interests of the sending State and its nationals, both individuals and bodies corporate, within the limits permitted by international law;
(b) furthering the development of commercial, economic, cultural and scientific relations between the sending State and the receiving State and otherwise promoting friendly relations between them [...];
(c) ascertaining by all lawful means conditions and developments in the commercial, economic, cultural and scientific life of the receiving State, reporting thereon to the Government of the sending State.'

A sending State must supply the head of a consular post with a commission (or similar instrument) relating to each appointment setting out, inter alia, his or her rank, the post's category, district, and seat.[24] It is also required to transmit such credentials to the government of the State in whose territory the head of a consular post is to exercise his or her functions.[25] If the receiving State decides to admit the head of the consular post to exercise his or her function in its territory it must grant an *exequatur* for this purpose.[26]

The 1932 Harvard Draft Convention on the Legal Position and Functions of Consuls suggested that a receiving State's decision to issue an *exequatur* admitting the head of a consular post constitutes an act from which recognition of the sending State (or its government) could be implied.[27] However, whether a sending State's request for an *exequatur* amounts to implied recognition of the receiving State is less clear. Special Rapporteur Zourek indicated that such a request would qualify as implied recognition.[28] In contrast, Lee and

23 The two categories of consular officers are 'career' and 'honorary': Article 1(2) VCCR. Heads of consular posts are ranked as follows: (a) consuls-general, (b) consuls, (c) vice-consuls, and (d) consular agents (Article 9(1) VCCR). A 'consular post' is defined as any (a) consulate-general, (b) consulate, (c) vice consulate, or (d) consular agency: Article 1(1)(a) VCCR.

24 Article 11(1) VCCR.

25 Article 11(2) VCCR. Or a notification of appointment containing the same particulars, if the receiving State is agreeable (Art 11(3) VCCR)

26 Article 12(1) VCCR. See Ivor Roberts (ed), *Satow's Diplomatic Practice* (7th ed, OUP 2017) 123. However, in practice, certain consular posts have been maintained despite the severing of diplomatic or consular relations.

27 Harvard 'Draft Convention on the Legal Position and Functions of Consuls' [1932] 26 *AJIL* Supp 193, 240, quoted in Lee and Quigley, *Consular Law and Practice* (3rd ed, OUP 2008) 68. Lauterpacht thought that the issuing of an *exequatur* 'probably' implied recognition of the sending State or government: (1947) at 406 (also cited in Lee and Quigley 68).

28 Jaroslav Zourek, UN ILC Special Rapporteur 'Report on Consular Intercourse and Immunities' (15 April 1957) [1957] vol II *UNYBILC* 71–103 (Art 12). UN Doc. A/CN.4/108, 15 April 1957. Cited in Lee & Quigley (n 27) 68. The ILC decided not to accept Zourek's proposal on this point.

Quigley argue that, as an *exequatur* is only granted in response to a request made by a sending State, the process of establishing a consulate gives rise to mutual recognition (when accompanied by an intention to recognise on the part of the sending and receiving States).[29] However, these scholars seem to have overlooked the unilateral character of recognition in this context. The pertinent issue is not the acts required to establish a consular post, but whether each State intends to recognise the other party.[30]

A degree of ambiguity persists about the precise relationship between the establishment of a consular post and the doctrine of recognition. Jennings and Watts followed Lauterpacht in thinking that recognition would 'probably' not be implied from the simple acts of the 'sending and reception of consuls (especially if [...] not accompanied by a request for or issue of an *exequatur*)'.[31] Lee and Quigley conclude that the question of whether the initiation of consular relations constitutes recognition is a matter of intention.[32] In the circumstances, it is apparent that the acts required to establish a consular post will only amount to implied recognition if they are supplemented by clear evidence of an intention to recognise on the part each State involved.[33]

Thus far, the focus has been on whether the opening of a consulate could amount to implied recognition of a State and/or government. However, the present enquiry concerns whether the establishment of a consulate could amount to implied recognition of a novel territorial claim asserted by an established State. It is, therefore, presupposed that the sending and receiving States already recognise one another. In this regard, Article 6(a) of the 1932 Harvard Draft Convention sets out the position from the sending State's perspective by indicating that:

> A sending State shall not be presumed to have recognised the authority in actual control of a territory as entitled to such control because it has appointed a person [...] to exercise consular functions within such territory.[34]

29 Lee and Quigley (n 27) 68. The authors add that the receiving State may decline to issue the requested *exequatur*. In fact, such a refusal is provided for in Article 12(2) VCCR.

30 See Thomas Grant, 'How to Recognise a State (and Not)' in Christine Chinkin and Freya Baetens (eds), *Sovereignty, Statehood and State Responsibility: Essays in Honour of James Crawford* (CUP 2013) 192–208, 200.

31 Arthur Watts and Robert Jennings (eds) *Oppenheim's International Law*, Vol. 1 (9th ed, OUP 1992) 146–147: quoted in Lee and Quigley (n 27) 68.

32 Lee and Quigley (n 27) 69. The present authors suggest that recognition is a unilateral act rather than a mutual process.

33 Such intention was clearly absent, for instance, in the case of Spain, which maintained a Consulate-General in Gibraltar from 1716 to 1954, despite never resiling from its claim to the territory: see Luis Romero Bartumeus, *El Consulado General de España en Gibraltar (1716-1954)* (2nd ed, Imagenta; Tarifa 2015).

34 Harvard Draft Convention 240, quoted in Lee and Quigley (n 27) 68.

The approach adopted by the UK government *vis-à-vis* Jerusalem after it had withdrawn from its role as the mandatory power of Palestine constitutes a useful case study of a consulate being established in a disputed territory without the sending State recognising the sovereignty claims of those authorities controlling the territory in issue.[35]

In 1948, the UK opened and operated a Consulate-General in Jerusalem without recognising Israel's claim to the city (both when it controlled only the western sector and when, after 1967, it also controlled eastern Jerusalem) or Jordan's claim during the time it controlled the city's eastern sector. Consequently, the UK did not transmit credentials, pursuant to a request for an *exequatur* for the Consuls-General it appointed to its Jerusalem consulate to either Israel or Jordan during this period, in keeping with its view that Jerusalem was not under the sovereignty of either State.[36] This case predated the VCCR's adoption and although the UK recognised both Jordan and Israel as States during this period, it did not consider either of them to be the 'receiving State' as far as Jerusalem was concerned. Accordingly, while this case is important for illustrative purposes, it is not directly comparable to the situation where sympathetic third States have opened consulates in occupied Western Sahara with Morocco's encouragement.

Despite the insights contained in the Harvard Draft Convention concerning the relationship between the founding of a consulate and recognition, it was produced over 90 years ago and much has happened in the intervening period, as far as the development of international law is concerned. Indeed, since the 1960s, the Security Council and the International Court of Justice (ICJ) have both embraced a broader conception of the relationship between diplomatic/consular relations and the doctrine of recognition. As discussed in Chapter 3(A), in its *Namibia* Advisory Opinion, the ICJ stipulated that any dealings between a third State and South Africa which may 'imply a recognition that South Africa's presence in Namibia is legal' would be inconsistent with the Security Council's declaration position in this context.[37] The Court went on to specify the requirements of this finding for member States, including the need to abstain from sending diplomatic and special missions to South Africa that included Namibia within their jurisdiction and from sending consular agents to Namibia, and the requirement to withdraw any such agents already in the Territory.[38] The Security Council itself has also taken decisive steps to bar or curtail diplomatic and/or consular representation in illegal situations which have triggered a duty of non-recognition. For example, it adopted resolution 217 (1965) through which it instructed third States

35 Lee and Quigley (n 27) 72.

36 ibid.

37 The Council's position was set out in paras 2 and 5 of SCR 276 (30 January 1970). See *Namibia* Advisory Opinion, paras 121 and 133. See Chapter III(A), above.

38 *Namibia* Advisory Opinion, para 123.

not to entertain diplomatic or other relations with the minority racist regime which then controlled Southern Rhodesia. Subsequently, the Council adopted resolution 253 (1968), by which it required all States to withdraw their consular representation from that country.[39] The above cases, which involved clear violations of *jus cogens* norms, suggest that the maintenance of consular relations presupposes the existence of ongoing mutual recognition. Accordingly, it would seem to follow that an instruction to withdraw consular representation, issued by the Security Council or ICJ, in a concrete situation, would be entirely consistent with the requirement of positive abstention generated by an established duty of non-recognition.

This development may indicate that the founding and operation of consulates in a territory claimed and controlled by a receiving State, in violation of peremptory norms of general international law, would be incompatible with the *erga omnes* obligations generated for all third States and IOs in such a context.[40] However, a more plausible reading is that it was not the duty of non-recognition under customary international law that validated the Security Council's specific instructions to member States to refrain from sending diplomatic and consular officials to the illegal situations prevailing in Namibia and Southern Rhodesia. Instead, the binding determinations made by the Security Council in relation to these illegal situations derived their authority from the powers conferred upon it by Article 25 of the UN Charter.[41] In the absence of such a Security Council decision, it should not be presumed that the establishment and maintenance of consular posts and diplomatic missions by third States and IOs in an unlawful territorial situation necessarily violates the duty of non-recognition.

The Territorial Foundations of Consular Representation

The territorial underpinnings of the consular relationship are evident from the VCCR's provisions. Article 4(1) provides that: 'A consular post may be established in the territory of the receiving State only with that State's consent'. Moreover, in relation to the process of appointing the head of a consular post, Article 11(2) stipulates that the sending State shall transmit the consular commission or instrument: 'to the Government of the State in whose territory the head of a consular post is to exercise his [her] functions'. Morocco's territorial expression is restricted to the territory over which it exercises lawful

39 SCR 217 (20 November 1965), adopted under Chapter VI and SCR 253 (29 May 1968), adopted pursuant to Chapter VII.

40 See chapter III(A), above.

41 This viewpoint is consistent with the interpretation offered by Judge Higgins in her Separate Opinion in the *Wall* Advisory Opinion, see paras 37–38. However, Talmon adopts a contrary approach. He endeavours to draw a distinction between the duty of non-recognition's content, and the measures adopted to satisfy that obligation. See (2005) at 112–113.

sovereignty.[42] Western Sahara does not constitute Moroccan territory as a matter of international law and, as a result, Morocco cannot be regarded as the receiving State as far as this Non-Self-Governing Territory (NSGT) is concerned. Morocco, therefore, cannot validly consent to the establishment of a consular post, by a third State, in Western Sahara, as anticipated by Article 4. Moreover, the procedure regarding the request or grant of an *exequatur*, as set out in Articles 11 and 12, cannot be fulfilled either. However, the above-mentioned VCCR provisions will be satisfied in relation to those third States which have established consulates in Western Sahara while manifesting a clear intention to recognise Morocco's sovereignty claim on the proviso that a duty of non-recognition has not been triggered as far as the situation in Western Sahara is concerned.

Arguably, the territorial connection is implicit in those consular functions enumerated in Article 5(a)–(c) of the VCCR.[43] It follows that a sending State cannot carry out consular functions unless it has established a consular post in the territory of the receiving State. This territorial link is also apparent from Article 30(1), which provides that: 'The receiving State shall either facilitate the acquisition on its territory [...] by the sending State of premises necessary for its consular post or assist the latter in the obtaining of accommodation in some other way'.[44] Article 34 adds that, subject to certain restrictions, 'the receiving State shall ensure freedom of movement and travel in its territory to all members of the consular post'. In the light of the above, any sending State would be in breach of the VCCR's provisions if it did not secure the consent of the lawful receiving State in connection with the opening and running of a consular post in that State's territory.

The recent spate of consulate openings in Morocco-controlled Western Sahara would appear to engage similar issues to those raised by Palestine in the ICJ proceedings it instituted against the USA concerning the relocation of its Israel embassy from Tel Aviv to Jerusalem.[45] In that case, Palestine argued that the USA was in violation of certain provisions of the Vienna Convention on Diplomatic Relations (VCDR) because its relocated embassy was no longer situated on Israel's territory. On 6 December 2017, President Trump made a public statement recognising Jerusalem as Israel's capital city while

42 In accordance with the terms of Article 29 of the VCLT. See, e.g., the CJEU's judgment in *Council v Polisario* (2016), paras 87–99.

43 A similar argument was made by Palestine in its Application of 28 September 2018 instituting ICJ proceedings against the USA in the *Relocation of the US Embassy to Jerusalem* Case in respect of the functions of a diplomatic mission as set out in Article 3 of the VCDR, 1961 (at paras 37–46): <https://www.icj-cij.org/sites/default/files/case-related/176/176-20180928-APP-01-00-EN.pdf> accessed 31 August 2023.

44 See the comparable provision in Article 21(1) VCDR, which was harnessed by Palestine in its 2018 application in the *Relocation of the US Embassy to Jerusalem* Case, para 43.

45 See Palestine's 2018 Application in the *Relocation of the US Embassy to Jerusalem* Case.

announcing an intention to relocate the US embassy there.[46] Subsequently, on 14 May 2018, the USA inaugurated its embassy in Jerusalem.[47] By taking such steps, the USA expressly recognised Israel's sovereignty claim to Jerusalem, whereas the present enquiry is focused on whether certain States have impliedly recognised Morocco's sovereignty claim to Western Sahara by opening consulates in that Territory. Accordingly, unlike in the *Relocation of the US Embassy* Case, the pivotal issue concerns recognition rather than whether such third States are in breach of the material treaty provisions by taking such steps.[48]

The VCDR manifests a strong territorial dimension, but it is possible that the geographical location of an embassy may not be as significant as Palestine asserted in the *Relocation of the US Embassy* Case because the existence of diplomatic relations does not necessarily require a sending State to establish a permanent mission in the receiving State.[49] Consular relations may also exist between two States in the absence of a consular post.[50] Nevertheless, third States have, in fact, chosen to establish physical consulates in Western Sahara and this book seeks to determine the consequences of this recent development for the recognition of Morocco's claim to this Territory. As discussed, the recognition of a territorial claim, asserted by a receiving State, by means of inaugurating a consulate in the disputed territory, can only be implied if this act is supplemented by evidence which evinces such an intention on the part of the sending State. The transmission of the necessary credentials for the appointed head of a consular post, by the sending State, or the issuing of an *exequatur* by the receiving State, would not be sufficient for this purpose. The key issue, therefore, is not whether Morocco recognises those third States that have chosen to inaugurate consulates in Western Sahara, so it does not matter whether the Moroccan government has issued an *exequatur* allowing a head of a consular post, appointed by the sending State in question, to be admitted for the purpose of carrying out his or her functions in 'its' territory. Such acts

46 ibid., para 21.

47 ibid., para 24.

48 The controversy surrounding the SADR's claim to statehood and the uncertain implications of Western Sahara's NSGT status as far as the VCCR is concerned as well as the consequences of the indispensable third-party rule (the Monetary Gold principle) for any potential litigation strategy combine to make such an approach deeply unattractive.

49 See Denza (n 22) 26–27. Diplomatic functions may be carried out in a variety of ways, including processes of multiple accreditation (Articles 5(2) and 6 VCDR); the use of occasional special missions and, in certain circumstances, the interests of a sending State can be protected by the diplomatic mission of a third State (Articles 45, 46 VCDR).

50 Article 4(1) VCCR provides that: 'A consular post may be established in the territory of the receiving State.' If consular relations have been severed, Article 27(1)(c) VCCR provides that a 'sending State may entrust the protection of its interests and those of its nationals to a third State acceptable to the receiving State'. See Lee and Quigley (n 27) 59–61 for a discussion of the practice adopted by British Commonwealth countries in cases where consular relations have been suspended.

would need to be accompanied by evidence that would be indicative of an intention to recognise Morocco's claim to Western Sahara on the part of the sending State in question. In the circumstances, a public statement made on behalf of the sending State either in the context of establishing a consulate in Western Sahara or in an international institution, such as the UN, may have probative value in this regard. An assessment would then need to be made as to whether such acts taken together reveal an intention to recognise impliedly Morocco's territorial claim to Western Sahara on the part of the sending State in issue.

Information relating to requests for an *exequatur* by the governments of third States in the context of establishing a consulate in Western Sahara and any concomitant grants thereof by the Moroccan government in compliance with the VCCR's provisions is not readily available. Despite the difficulty in gaining access to such documentation, it may be significant that the Moroccan government has arranged for inauguration ceremonies to be held to mark the occasion of the opening of each consulate in Western Sahara. Such formal events have been invariably co-chaired by the Moroccan Foreign Minister and either the sending State's Foreign Minister or its Ambassador to Morocco, and accompanied by statements of Morocco's position *vis-à-vis* its 'southern provinces', and the standpoint of the sending State on this issue.[51] These events have been reported both within the Moroccan media and internationally. It is pertinent to examine material statements made by the representatives of sending States in the context of establishing consulates in Western Sahara, along with relevant statements made by the representatives of such States in international fora such as the UN, and to consider what such statements may reveal about the intentions of these States *vis-à-vis* the recognition of Morocco's claim to Western Sahara.

As discussed earlier in this chapter, the USA's current position on the status of Western Sahara was set out in a presidential proclamation issued, on 10 December 2010, by President Trump. It is worth quoting from this proclamation at length:

> [T]he United States recognizes Moroccan sovereignty over the entire Western Sahara territory and reaffirms its support for Morocco's serious, credible, and realistic autonomy proposal as the only basis for a just and lasting solution to the dispute over the Western Sahara territory [...] We urge the parties to engage in discussions without delay, using Morocco's autonomy plan as the only framework to negotiate a mutually acceptable

51 Such inauguration ceremonies have been reported by *Morocco World News*. See, e.g., 'Jordan Officially Opens Consulate in Morocco's Laayoune', *Morocco World News*, 4 March 2021, <https://www.moroccoworldnews.com/2021/03/336541/jordan-officially-opens-consulate-in-moroccos-laayoune> accessed 31 August 2023.

> solution. To facilitate progress toward this aim, the United States will encourage economic and social development with Morocco, including in the Western Sahara territory, and to that end will open a consulate in the Western Sahara territory, in Dakhla, to promote economic and business opportunities for the region.[52]

Rather than signalling an end to the USA's commitment to the UN's political process regarding Western Sahara, the Trump administration insisted that it remained committed to a negotiated solution.[53] Regarding the establishment of a consulate in Western Sahara, the USA's Ambassador to Morocco explained, on 24 December 2020, that:

> In the weeks ahead, we will initiate the process of identifying an appropriate site for a physical consulate. Opening a consulate will allow the United States to take further advantage of Morocco's strategic positioning as a hub for trade in Africa, Europe, and the Middle East. Specifically, it will support and encourage investment and development projects that bring tangible benefits for the region. In the meantime, this Virtual Presence Post for Western Sahara represents our commitment to strengthening our already strong ties with Morocco, built over 200 years of friendship.[54]

The Trump administration encountered difficulties in securing congressional funding for the purpose of opening a consulate in Western Sahara.[55] Consequently, the virtual presence post remains operational for the time being.

Having chosen to establish consulates in Western Sahara, several third States made statements in support of Morocco's sovereignty claim to the Territory. For instance, on 4 November 2020, Sheikh Abdullah bin Zayed Al Nahyan, the UAE's Foreign Minister, announced that his country had opened a Consulate General in Laayoune 'in the southern provinces of the Kingdom of Morocco'.[56] He explained that this decision reflected the UAE's long-standing relationship with Morocco, which was 'strengthened by the

52 'Proclamation on Recognizing the Sovereignty of the Kingdom Of Morocco Over the Western Sahara' – US Embassy & Consulates in Morocco (usembassy.gov).

53 See White House Press Statement, 11 December 2020: 'President Donald J. Trump Has Brokered Peace Between Israel and the Kingdom of Morocco' – The White House (archives.gov). The Biden administration has not sought to resile from this policy approach since assuming office.

54 'Virtual Presence Post for Western Sahara' – US Embassy and Consulates in Morocco (usembassy.gov).

55 <https://foreignpolicy.com/2022/01/04/morocco-diplomacy-bourita-united-states-western-sahara-2022-budget/> accessed 31 August 2023.

56 'UAE Opens Consulate in Moroccan City of Laayoune' (mofaic.gov.ae) accessed 31 August 2023.

UAE's participation in the "Green March"'.[57] Further, during a ministerial conference organised by the USA and Morocco, held on 15 January 2021, the UAE's Foreign Minister confirmed:

> [T]he principled and firm position of the United Arab Emirates in support of the sisterly Kingdom of Morocco [regarding] the status of the Moroccan Sahara where the UAE reaffirms its full support for Morocco's sovereignty over this entire region and for all the measures taken by the Kingdom to defend its territorial integrity and the security of its citizens.[58]

During a C24 meeting, held on 14 June 2021, the UAE's representative reiterated that: 'his Government fully supported the sovereignty of Morocco over all the Moroccan Sahara' and that it had established a consulate in 'the Moroccan city of Laayoune'.[59] Subsequently, on 27 October 2022, during the Security Council meeting at which resolution 2654 was adopted, the UAE offered its 'full support for the Kingdom of Morocco and its sovereignty over the entire Moroccan Sahara'.[60] Its representative also advocated in favour of Morocco's autonomy initiative, which 'is in line with the Charter of the United Nations and the Organization's resolutions and preserves Morocco's territorial integrity' in his country's opinion.[61]

On 27 November 2020, Bahrain's Ambassador to Morocco publicly confirmed his country's decision to establish a Consulate General in Laayoune adding that this step, 'is a reflection of Bahrain's position in support of the territorial integrity and national unity of Morocco'.[62] The foreign ministers of Morocco and Bahrain attended an inauguration ceremony at which Bahrain's Consulate General in Laayoune was officially opened on 14 December 2020.[63] Subsequently, during a C24 meeting, Bahrain's representative informed the Special Committee that her country had established a consulate in Laayoune while expressing Bahrain's support for Morocco's 'serious and credible efforts to achieve a political solution to the question of the Moroccan Sahara through its autonomy initiative, which [...] was in compliance with the

57 ibid.

58 H.H. Sheikh Abdullah bin Zayed: 'We re-affirm our support for Kingdom of Morocco's sovereignty over entire region of Moroccan Sahara' (mofaic.gov.ae)

59 Third Meeting C24, 14 June 2021, PM, A/AC.109/2021/SR.3 [49].

60 S/PV. 9168, p 3. The UAE's representative also observed that the Council considers this proposal to be 'serious and credible' as apparent from its resolutions on this issue.

61 ibid.

62 News Details: Ambassador of Bahrain in Rabat confirms that decision of Bahrain to open Consulate General in El-Ayoun City reflects continuous support of Bahrain to Morocco (mofa.gov.bh).

63 'Bahrain Opens Consulate General in Laayoune, Southern Morocco' (moroccoworldnews.com).

relevant Security Council resolutions and respected the sovereignty, unity and territorial integrity of Morocco'.[64]

During the 2020 proceedings of the Fourth Committee, Comoros, Equatorial Guinea, São Tomé and Príncipe, and Guinea-Bissau all informed the Committee that they had recently inaugurated consulates in either Laayoune or Dakhla in Western Sahara.[65] The Comorian representative said that his government also supported the UN-led process to find a mutually acceptable solution to the 'question of Moroccan Sahara' while asserting that Morocco's autonomy initiative was consistent with the UN Charter, the relevant UN resolutions, and international law.[66] Equatorial Guinea's representative addressed the 'question of Moroccan Sahara' by praising the significant steps that Morocco had already taken, within the framework of its autonomy initiative, to develop 'the country's southern provinces'.[67] He expressed his government's gratitude for the assistance provided by the Moroccan government in relation to its opening of a consulate in Dakhla.[68] São Tomé and Príncipe's representative declared that his country had opened a consulate in Laayoune 'in recognition of the territorial integrity of Morocco'.[69] Moreover, Guinea-Bissau's representative expressed her country's support for Morocco's autonomy initiative, adding that Morocco's regional investment strategy had encouraged it to open a consulate in Dakhla.[70]

During a C24 meeting, held on 14 June 2021, Gambia's representative stated that: 'His Government supported the right of Morocco to sovereignty and territorial integrity, including in relation to the Moroccan Sahara, and had established a consulate in Dakhla, Moroccan Sahara, in 2020'.[71] On the same occasion, Djibouti's representative informed the Special Committee that his country had established a consulate in Dakhla in February 2020 while expressing the view that: 'the Moroccan autonomy initiative provided an excellent basis for negotiations'.[72] Jordan's representative said that 'his Government supported the right of Morocco to territorial integrity and had

64 Third Meeting C24, 14 June 2021, PM, A/AC.109/2021/SR.3 [44].

65 See the statement made by representatives of the Comoros and Equatorial Guinea, Fourth Committee, 7th meeting, 23 October 2020, A/C.4/75/SR.7 [58-59] and [60]; Sao Tome & Principe and Guinea-Bissau, Fourth Committee, 8th meeting, 3 November 2020, A/C.4/75/SR.8 [32] and [70].

66 See statement made by representative of the Comoros, Fourth Committee, 7th meeting, 23 October 2020, A/C.4/75/SR.7 [58-59].

67 See the statement made by representative of Equatorial Guinea, Fourth Committee, 7th meeting, 23 October 2020, A/C.4/75/SR.7 [60].

68 See the statement made by representative of Equatorial Guinea, Fourth Committee, 7th meeting, 23 October 2020, A/C.4/75/SR.7 [60].

69 See the statement made by representative of São Tomé and Príncipe and Guinea-Bissau, Fourth Committee, 8th meeting, 3 November 2020, A/C.4/75/SR.8 [32].

70 See the statement made by representative of Guinea-Bissau, 8th meeting, 3 November 2020, A/C.4/75/SR.8 [70].

71 Third Meeting C24, 14 June 2021, PM, A/AC.109/2021/SR.3 [19].

72 ibid., para 27.

recently established a consulate in the Moroccan city of Laayoune'.[73] Burkina Faso's representative also endorsed Morocco's autonomy initiative saying that it was 'a credible and realistic proposal', he also mentioned that his country had opened a consulate in Dakhla.[74] Senegal's representative declared his country's support for Morocco's autonomy initiative while applauding it for fostering human rights and socio-economic development 'in the Moroccan Sahara' leading Senegal to open a consulate in Dakhla in April 2021.[75] On 21 July 2022, Togo opened a consulate in Dakhla at an inauguration ceremony attended by Morocco's Foreign Minister and his Togolese counterpart.[76] Prior to this step, Togo's Foreign Minister reassured Morocco of Togo's support 'for the pursuit of a lasting solution that preserves the territorial integrity unity and sovereignty of the Kingdom of Morocco under the exclusive aegis of the UN'.[77]

Despite such strong and direct support for Morocco's sovereignty claim to Western Sahara, most States opening consulates in Western Sahara have only been willing to endorse Morocco's autonomy plan, thereby offering indirect support for its claim. For instance, on 19 December 2020, Congo opened a consulate in Dakhla, while declaring its support for Morocco's autonomy plan.[78] Further, the Central African Republic's Foreign Minister reaffirmed her country's support for Morocco's autonomy plan during a joint press briefing held with Morocco's Foreign Minister on 12 May 2022, 'as the one and only solution within the framework of its territorial integrity'.[79] Suriname, which established a consulate in Dakhla on 26 May 2022, expressed its support for Morocco's autonomy plan as a unique and consensual basis for settling the dispute.[80] On 31 March 2022, Dominica's Prime Minister attended an inauguration ceremony at which he opened a Consulate General in Dakhla on behalf of the six members of the Organization of the Eastern Caribbean States.[81] On this occasion, he expressed his country's full support for Morocco's

73 ibid., para 28.

74 ibid., paras 32–33.

75 Ibid., paras 51–52.

76 'Togo Officially Opens Consulate General in Morocco's Dakhla' (moroccoworldnews.com).

77 The Foreign Ministers of Morocco and Togo met in Rabat on 7 June 2022 during the first ministerial meeting of the African Atlantic States: 'Togo to Open a Consulate in Dakhla' – République Togolaise (republicoftogo.com).

78 'Western Sahara: DR Congo Opens Consulate General in Dakhla' (moroccoworldnews.com).

79 The Central African Republic opened a consulate in Laayoune in January 2020: 'Central African Republic Renews Support for Morocco's Autonomy Plan' (moroccoworldnews.com).

80 'Suriname To Open Consulate General in Morocco's Dakhla Thursday' (moroccoworldnews .com).

81 'Eastern Caribbean states open consulate in Western Sahara' (Reuters, 21 March 2022). More generally, see: Nand Bardouille, 'Turning to Rabat: Explaining the Elevation of Moroccan Relations with Caribbean Countries' (2022) 57 *The International Spectator* 121–140.

autonomy plan as a unique and consensual solution to the dispute.[82] Cabo Verde established a consulate in Dakhla on 31 August 2022. In June 2022, its Foreign Minister stated that Morocco's autonomy plan represents the most credible and realistic way of ending the dispute.[83] On 27 October 2022, during the Security Council meeting at which resolution 2654 was adopted, Gabon explained that it supported the UN process of finding 'a realistic, feasible and lasting political solution'.[84] Gabon's representative said that his country's vote reflected its 'support for Morocco's autonomy plan, which presents credible and reassuring prospects that allow not only for a way out of the current impasse but also for a mutually acceptable political solution to be reached'.[85]

It appears that many of the States which have established consulates in Western Sahara prefer to endorse Morocco's autonomy plan in the context of the UN-facilitated political process concerning the Western Sahara Question, rather than addressing the sovereignty question overtly. This approach has the advantage of drawing cover from the international community's institutional initiative, despite its drift towards a solution that is at odds with international legality, while pleasing Morocco since it is willing to make explicit the connection between support, from third States, for its autonomy plan for Western Sahara and the supposed preservation of its territorial integrity. The available evidence supports the view that several States have impliedly recognised Morocco's sovereignty claim to Western Sahara as not only have they established consulates in Western Sahara, but they have also made unequivocal public statements expressing the view that Morocco exercises sovereignty over Western Sahara, thereby evincing an intention to recognise Morocco's claim to this Territory by implication. States falling within this category appear to include: the UAE, Bahrain, Comoros, Equatorial Guinea, São Tomé and Príncipe, Guinea-Bissau, Gambia, Jordan, Burkina Faso, Senegal, and Togo. Nonetheless, the positions adopted by most States that have established consulates in Western Sahara so far do not reveal a clear intention to recognise Morocco's claim impliedly. Instead, these States have garnered a benefit from the blurring of international legality and political reality which has characterised the UN's approach to Western Sahara in recent years. Nevertheless, a clear trend in favour of recognising Morocco's claim is emerging and when this is combined with growing support for Morocco's autonomy plan across the international community, and the ambiguities apparent within the UN's current approach to the Western Sahara Question, it is hard to see how the

82 'Organization of Eastern Caribbean States Opens Consulate General in Dakhla' (moroccoembassy.vn).

83 'Cape Verde Officially Opens Consulate in Morocco's Dakhla' (moroccoworldnews.com); and 'Inauguration of the Consulate-General of the Republic of Cabo Verde in Dakhla' – Ministry of Foreign Affairs, African Cooperation and Moroccan Expatriates (diplomatie.ma).

84 S/PV.9168, p 5.

85 ibid.

international legal principles associated with decolonisation are being upheld in such a setting.

Morocco's autonomy proposal and its emergent policy of encouraging third States to establish consulates in Western Sahara are undoubtedly significant elements of its recognition strategy as far as its sovereignty claim to 'its southern provinces' is concerned. Indeed, it is hard to overstate the importance of the recent developments discussed in this chapter for the Moroccan government. In fact, the government's interpretation of such events was apparent from a speech given by King Mohammed VI, on 29 July 2023, on the 24th anniversary of his accession to the throne. He drew attention to the magnitude of a: 'series of decisions to recognize Morocco's sovereignty over its southern provinces – the latest being that of the State of Israel – as well as to open consulates in Laayoune and Dakhla, not to mention the growing support for the Autonomy Initiative'.[86] In the circumstances, the final chapter of this book will reflect on whether Morocco is now in the process of acquiring good title to Western Sahara in keeping with the principle of *ex factis jus oritur* (the law arises from the facts) and at the expense of the principle of *ex injuria jus non oritur* (unlawful acts cannot create law). In so doing, it examines what such a potential outcome might reveal about the content and operation of the doctrines of self-determination and recognition in contemporary international law.

86 Quoted by the UN Secretary-General in his latest Report on the situation in Western Sahara, S/2023/729 (3 October 2023) para 25. On 17 July 2023, the Israeli Prime Minister announced Israel's decision, 'to recognize the sovereignty of Morocco over the territory of Western Sahara' along with its intention to consider establishing a consulate in Dakhla (para 24).

6 Conclusion

The Future of Western Sahara and the Future of International Law

Despite a small number of countervailing examples,[1] the politics of recognition, and accompanying perceptions of the viability of Morocco's autonomy plan, appear to be shifting in Morocco's favour. By contrast, the law on self-determination and territorial integrity – at least as interpreted by the International Court of Justice (ICJ) – has not shifted. If anything, since the *Chagos* Advisory Opinion, the applicable principles – especially the requirement to respect the territorial integrity of Non-Self-Governing Territories (NSGTs) as a corollary of the right to self-determination – are now even more brightly drawn than they were when the ICJ held in 1975 that the exercise of the right of self-determination of the Sahrawi people could not be displaced by Morocco's territorial claim.[2] At the time of writing, it remains to be seen what the ICJ will decide in its second advisory opinion on Palestine, but it is unlikely to dilute the principle that unlawful occupation cannot subvert the right to self-determination or the obligations on third States to uphold that

1 E.g., Peru re-established diplomatic relations with SADR on 8 September 2021. It had recognised the Sahrawi Arab Democratic Republic (SADR) in 1984 and then purported to freeze recognition in 1996: <https://www.gob.pe/institucion/rree/noticias/521117-restablecimiento-de-relaciones-diplomaticas-con-la-rasd> accessed 31 August 2023. Writing in 2008, Ricardo Sánchez Serra <http://rsanchezserra.blogspot.com/2008/12/el-estoicismo-del-pueblo-saharaui.html > (accessed 31 August 2023) describes the 'extremely strange' decision to 'freeze' recognition on 9 September 1996, putting it down to Moroccan lobbying, and describes initiatives from 2005 onwards to get Peru to re-establish relations with the SADR, including a joint letter by Peruvian presidential candidates on 24 October 2005. The UK has also recently demurred from offering its support to the Moroccan autonomy plan, and referred to the UK's 'longstanding position on Western Sahara in support of the UN resolutions and the importance of principles, including self-determination', in a UK–Morocco Joint Declaration of 9 May 2023, adopted in the context of the UK–Morocco Association Agreement: <https://www.gov.uk/government/publications/morocco-uk-strategic-dialogue-session-4-joint-declaration-2023/fourth-session-of-the-moroccan-uk-strategic-dialogue-and-second-session-of-the-association-council-of-the-uk-morocco-association-agreement-joint-decl> (paras 7–9), accessed 31 August 2023.

2 *Legal Consequences of the Separation of the Chagos Archipelago from Mauritius in 1965* [2019] *ICJ Rep* 95. The Court affirmed that, in accordance with consistent State practice, 'respect for the territorial integrity of a non-self-governing territory is a key element of the exercise of the right to self-determination under international law' (para 160). See Stephen Allen, 'Self-determination, the *Chagos Advisory Opinion* and the Chagossians' (2020) 69 *ICLQ* 203–220.

DOI: 10.4324/9781032658827-6

right.[3] A multilateral endorsement of the Moroccan autonomy plan without Sahrawi support would therefore be impossible to reconcile with international law as it currently stands, and the resulting systemic dissonance would need to be resolved through the usual process of contestation. It would not be the first time that decolonisation practice appears out of step with decolonisation norms (consider, for example, the reactions of States to the forceful annexation by India of the Portuguese NSGTs of Goa, Daman, and Diu in 1961, or to the Indonesian occupation of East Timor).[4] Attempts to rationalise the denial of self-determination in NSGTs with covetous neighbours tend to maintain either that the rules were abandoned exceptionally in favour of political pragmatism, or that the outcome fits with an interpretation of the existing rules.[5] Morocco will likely maintain that an endorsement of its autonomy plan is consistent with, rather than a departure from, the existing rules, just as many of its supporters have already sought to justify their position by reference to the UN process, or Morocco's 'territorial integrity'.

In the immediate wake of the ICJ's *Western Sahara* Opinion, the Moroccan Mission at the UN stated that:

> the opinion of the Court can only mean one thing: the so-called Western Sahara was part of Moroccan territory over which the sovereignty was exercised by the King of Morocco and that the population of this territory considered themselves and were considered to be Moroccans.[6]

This is, of course, the opposite of what the ICJ held. Franck, describing the Moroccan statement as 'worthy of the perverse Red Queen in Lewis Caroll's *Through the Looking Glass*', expressed concern regarding the creation of a 'precedent with a potential for future mischief' if Morocco got its way and Western Sahara was denied self-determination.[7]

A difference between today and 1976, when Franck was writing, is that there are now far fewer territories awaiting (formal) decolonisation.[8] The handful of hard cases that remain, like Western Sahara, have proved so

3 *Legal Consequences arising from the Policies and Practices of Israel in the Occupied Palestinian Territory, including East Jerusalem*, request for Advisory Opinion transmitted to the Court by UNGA Res 77/247 (30 December 2022).

4 Jamie Trinidad, *Self-Determination in Disputed Colonial Territories* (CUP 2018) 157 et seq.

5 See ibid., for evidence of both types of argument being used to rationalise the setting aside of self-determination in, inter alia, the French and Portuguese exclaves in India, Ifni, and Gibraltar.

6 Press release of the Permanent Mission of Morocco to the UN, 16 October 1975, quoted in UN Doc S/PV.1849 (1975) 11.

7 Thomas Franck, 'The Stealing of the Sahara' (1976) 70 *AJIL* 694, 711.

8 At the time of writing, 17 territories – including Western Sahara – remain on the UN Committee of 24's list of NSGTs, down from a peak of 72 in 1946: <https://www.un.org/dppa/decolonization/en/nsgt> accessed 31 August 2023. Since 1975, some 27 territories have been removed from the C24's list, and only one territory – Timor Leste – has been decolonised since the turn of

intractable that States may be more receptive to piecemeal 'pragmatic' solutions, and less fazed by concerns surrounding the unintended consequences of rule breaking.

Against this, it could be said that the ICJ, as the principal judicial organ of the UN, continues to fulfil a role of special significance when ruling on UN-generated law (in this case, the principles of self-determination and territorial integrity that underpin not only the decolonisation process but also, in a broader sense, the modern international legal order).[9] For as long as the ICJ 'holds the line' on the sanctity of these principles and the duty of non-recognition in respect of situations that breach them, it will be difficult for anyone to argue that the international law in this area is changing with the facts on the ground. This is especially true while Morocco and many of its supporters maintain that their preferred outcome would be entirely compatible with the law of decolonisation as it has existed since at least 1960, rather than a breach of that law or a reflection of its evolving character. In other words, they are not openly pushing the normative envelope; they are trying to dress up their preferred outcome as compliant with the existing rules system.[10]

An internationally approved settlement of the future status of Western Sahara could nevertheless turn out to be a pivotal moment in the UN era. If the use of force in violation of the UN Charter is allowed to prevail over the right to self-determination, knock-on effects of the sort feared by Franck in 1976 could well materialise, with catastrophic consequences in places like Palestine and Ukraine.[11] The Western Sahara Question may not be at the top

---

the millennium: <https://www.un.org/dppa/decolonization/en/history/former-trust-and-nsgts> accessed 31 August 2023.

9 In the wake of the *Chagos* Advisory Opinion, the ICJ will have opportunities to cast further light on the state of the law when it considers the territorial status of two former NSGTs (in *Arbitral Award of 3 October 1899 (Guyana/Venezuela)* and *Guatemala's Territorial, Insular and Maritime Claim (Guatemala/Belize)*) and the former Trust Territory of Palestine (*Legal Consequences Arising from the Policies and Practices of Israel in the Occupied Palestinian Territory, Including East Jerusalem*).

10 As Karen Knop observes in relation to the *Western Sahara* advisory proceedings, 'Morocco and Mauritania both argued that the conflict between the right of the Western Saharan population to choose their future political status and the restoration of Morocco's and Mauritania's territorial integrity was a conflict within the modern international legal rules on self-determination': *Diversity and Self-Determination in International Law* (CUP 2002) 159.

11 It is noteworthy that on the eve of the Russian invasion of Ukraine, President Biden – who has so far upheld his predecessor's policy of recognising Moroccan sovereignty over Western Sahara – made a staunch defence of the right of 'nations' to 'sovereignty and territorial integrity'; 'They have the freedom to set their own course and choose with whom they will associate': White House Press Briefing, 'Remarks by President Biden Providing an Update on Russia and Ukraine' (16 February 2022), <https://www.whitehouse.gov/briefing-room/speeches-remarks/2022/02/15/remarks-by-president-biden-providing-an-update-on-russia-and-ukraine/> accessed 31 August 2023. Ukraine, for its part, has endorsed the Moroccan autonomy plan. During a visit to Rabat on 22 May 2023, the Ukrainian Foreign Minister described the plan as 'a serious and credible basis for a successful resolution to the Sahara issue', while affirming his country's support for

of the international agenda, but it has the potential to shake the legal and political architecture of the UN order to its foundations. In years to come, the treatment of Western Sahara could yet come to be seen as an important turning point for the future of international law.

the efforts of the UN Secretary General's Representative, and describing the principle of territorial integrity as 'an absolutely sacred concept': 'Ukrainian and Moroccan FMs meet in Rabat' (Africanews, 23 May 2023, <https://www.africanews.com/2023/05/22/ukrainian-and-moroccan-fms-meet-in-rabat//> accessed 22 November 2023).

Index

Made in the USA
Las Vegas, NV
19 September 2026

e4021e27-0a02-479d-a180-7e82a0fbd692R02